KINGS, CHRONICLES, EZRA, NEHEMIAH, ESTHER

KINGS, CHRONICLES, EZRA, NEHEMIAH, ESTHER
God Rules His People

LEAFWOOD
PUBLISHERS
an imprint of Abilene Christian University Press

ISBN 978-1-68426-437-7

Printed in the United States of America

Library of Congress Cataloging-in-Publication Data

Cover design by Bruce Gore | Interior text design by Sandy Armstrong, Strong Design

Leafwood Publishers is an imprint of Abilene Christian University Press.
ACU Box 29138
Abilene, Texas 79699

1-877-816-4455
www.leafwoodpublishers.com

24 25 26 27 28 29 30 / 7 6 5 4 3 2 1

A MEDITATIVE COMMENTARY *on the Old Testament*

KINGS, CHRONICLES, EZRA, NEHEMIAH, ESTHER

GOD RULES HIS PEOPLE

GARY HOLLOWAY

LEAFWOOD PUBLISHERS
an imprint of Abilene Christian University Press

To Paula and Rick Marrs

CONTENTS

INTRODUCTION

HEARING GOD IN SCRIPTURE

There are many commentaries, guides, and workbooks on the various books of the Bible. How is this series different? It is not intended to answer all your scholarly questions about the Bible, or even make you an expert in the details of Scripture. Instead, this series is designed to help you hear the voice of God for your everyday life. It is a guide to meditation on the Bible, meditation that will allow the Bible to transform you.

We read in many ways. We might scan the newspaper for information, read a map for location, read a novel for pleasure, or read a textbook to pass a test. These are all good ways to read, depending on our circumstances.

A young soldier far away from home who receives a letter from his wife reads in yet another way. He might scan the letter quickly at first for news and information. But his longing for his beloved causes him to read the letter again and again, hearing her sweet voice in every line. He slowly treasures each word of this precious letter.

Bible Study

So also, there are many good ways to read the Bible, depending on our circumstances. Bible study is absolutely necessary for our life with God. We rightly study the Bible for information. We ask: Who wrote this? When was it written? Who were the original readers? How do these words apply to me? More importantly, we want information about God. Who is he? What does he think of me? What does he want from me?

There is no substitute for this kind of close, dedicated Bible study. We must know what the Bible says to know our standing with God. We therefore read the Bible to discover true doctrine or teaching. But some in their emphasis on the authority and inspiration of the Bible have forgotten that Bible study is not an end in itself. We want to know God through Scripture. We want to have a relationship with the Teacher, not just the teachings.

Jesus tells some of God's people in his day, "You study the Scriptures diligently because you think that in them you have eternal life. These are the very Scriptures that testify about me, yet you refuse to come to me to have life" (John 5:39–40 NIV). He's not telling them to study their Bibles less, but he is reminding them of the deeper purpose of Bible study—to draw us to God through Jesus. Bible study is a means, not an end.

Yet the way many of us have learned to study the Bible may actually get in the way of hearing God. "Bible study" may sound a lot like schoolwork, and many of us were happy to get out of school. "Bible study" may call to mind pictures of intellectuals surrounded by books in Greek and Hebrew, pondering meanings too deep for ordinary people. The method of Bible study that has been popular for some time focuses on the strangeness of the Bible. It was written long ago, far away, and in languages we cannot read. There is a huge gap between us and the original readers of the Bible, a gap that can only be bridged by scholars, not by average folk.

There is some truth and some value in that "scholarly" method. It is true that the Bible was not written originally to us. Knowing ancient languages and customs can at times help us understand the Bible better. However, one unintended result of this approach is to make the Bible distant from the people of God. We may come to think that we can only hear God indirectly through Scripture, that his Word must be filtered through scholars. We may even think that deep Bible study is a matter of mastering obscure information about the Bible.

Meditation

But we read the Bible for more than information. By studying it, we experience transformation, the mysterious process of God at work in us. Through his loving words, God is calling us to life with him. He is forming us into the image of his Son.

Reading the Bible is not like reading other books. We are not simply trying to learn information or master material. Instead, we want to stand under the authority of Scripture and let God master us. While we read the Bible, it reads us, opening the depths of our being to the overpowering love of God. "For the word of God is alive and active. Sharper than any double-edged sword, it penetrates even to dividing soul and spirit, joints and marrow; it judges the thoughts and attitudes of the heart. Nothing in all creation is hidden from God's sight. Everything is uncovered and laid bare before the eyes of him to whom we must give account" (Heb. 4:12–13 NIV).

Opening our hearts to the Word of God is meditation. Although this way of reading the Bible may be new to some, it has a long heritage among God's people. The psalmist joyously meditates on the words of God (Ps. 1:2; 39:3; 119:15, 23, 27, 48, 78, 97, 99, 148). Meditation is taking the words of Scripture to heart and letting them ask questions of us. It is slowing down, chewing over a text, listening closely, reading God's message of love to us over and over. This is not a simple, easy, or naïve reading of Scripture, but a process that takes time, dedication, and practice on our part.

There are many ways to meditate on the Bible. One is praying the Scriptures. Prayer and Bible study cannot be separated. One way of praying the Bible is to make the words of a text your prayer. Obviously, the prayer texts of Scripture, especially the Psalms, lend themselves to this. "The LORD is my shepherd" has been the prayer of many hearts.

However, it is proper and helpful to turn the words of the Bible into prayers. Commands from God can become prayers. "You shall have no other gods before me" (Exod. 20:3 NIV) can be prayed, "Lord, keep me from anything that takes your place in my heart." Stories can be prayed. Jesus heals a man born blind (John 9), and so we pray, "Lord Jesus, open my eyes to who you truly are." Even the promises of the Bible become prayers. "Never will I leave you; never will I forsake you" (Heb. 13:5 NIV; see Deut. 31:6) becomes, "God, help me know your promise that you are always with me so I may live my life without fear."

Obviously, there are many helpful ways of hearing the voice of God in Scripture. Again, the purpose of Bible reading and study is not to know more about the Bible, much less to pride ourselves as experts on Scripture; instead, we read to hear the voice of our Beloved—we listen for a word of God for us.

Holy Reading

This commentary reflects one ancient way of meditation and praying the Scriptures known as *lectio divina*, or "holy reading." This method assumes that God wants to speak to us directly in the Bible, that the passage we are reading is God's Word to us right now. The writers of the New Testament read the Old Testament with this same conviction. They saw the words of the Bible speaking directly to their own situations. They read with humility and with prayer.

The first step along this way of holy reading is listening to the Bible. Choose a biblical text that is not too long. It is helpful to hear Scripture in various translations. The passages in this commentary alternate among the New International Version, the New Living Translation, and the English Standard Version. *Note that this book will not look at every verse in 1 and 2 Kings, 1 and 2 Chronicles, Ezra, Nehemiah, or Esther.* You may not find a meditation here on your favorite verse. The purpose is to hear God's voice in your current situation, not to cover material or prepare lessons. Get into a comfortable position and maintain silence before God for several minutes. This prepares the heart to listen. Read slowly. Savor each word. Perhaps read aloud. Listen for a particular phrase that speaks to you. Ask God, What are you trying to tell me today?

The next step is to meditate on that phrase. That meditation may include slowly repeating the phrase that seems to be for you today. As you think deeply on it, you might even memorize it. Committing biblical passages to memory allows us to hold them in our hearts all day long. If you keep a journal, you might write the passage there. Let those words sink deeply into your heart.

Then pray those words back to God in your heart. Those words may call up visual images, smells, sounds, and feelings. Pay attention to what God is giving you in those words. Then respond in faith to what those words say to your heart. What do they call you to be and to do? Our humble response might take the form of praise, thanksgiving, joy, confession, or even cries of pain.

The final step in this "holy reading" is contemplation of God. The words from God that we receive deeply in our hearts lead us to him. Through these words, we experience union with the all-powerful God of love. Again, one should not separate Bible reading from prayer. The words of God in Scripture transport us into the very presence of God where we joyfully rest in his love.

What keeps reading the Bible this way from becoming merely our own desires read back into Scripture? How do we know it is God's voice we hear and not our own?

Two things. One is prayer. We are asking God to open our hearts, minds, and lives to him. We ask to hear his voice—not ours nor the voice of the world around us.

The second thing that keeps this from being an exercise in self-deception is to study the Bible in community. By praying over Scripture in a group, we hear God's Word together. God speaks through the other members of our group. The wisdom he gives them keeps us from private, selfish, and unusual interpretations. They help us keep our own voices in check as we desire to listen to God alone.

How to Use This Commentary

This commentary assists us in holy reading of the Bible. It gives structure to daily personal devotions, family meditation, small group Bible studies, and church classes.

Daily Devotional

Listening, meditation, prayer, contemplation. How does this commentary fit into this way of Bible study? Consider it as a conversation partner. We have taken a section of Scripture and then broken it down into four short daily readings. After listening, meditating, praying, and contemplating the passage for the day, use the questions suggested in the commentary to provoke deeper reflection. This provides a structure for a daily fifteen-minute devotional four days a week. On the fifth day, read the entire passage, meditate, and then use the questions to reflect on the meaning of the whole scripture. On day six, explore a series of meditations on the passage, which you can treat like conversation with another who has prayed over the text.

If you want to begin daily Bible reading but need guidance, this provides a Monday through Saturday experience that prepares the heart for worship and praise on Sunday. This structure also results in a communal reading of Scripture, instead of a private reading. Even if you use this commentary alone, you are not reading privately. God is at work in you and in the conversation you have with another (the author of the commentary) who has sought to hear God through this passage of the Bible.

Family Bible Study

This commentary can also provide an arrangement for family Bible study. Many Christian parents want to lead their children in daily study but don't know where to begin or how to structure their time. Using the six-day plan outlined above means the entire family can read, meditate, pray, and reflect on the shorter passages, using the questions provided. On day five, your family can review the entire passage, and then on day six, read the meditations in the commentary to prompt reflection and discussion. God will bless our families beyond our imaginations through the prayerful study of his Word.

Weekly Group Study

This commentary can also structure small group Bible study. Each member of the group should have meditated over the daily readings and questions for the five days preceding the group meeting, using the method outlined above. The day before the group meeting, each member should read and reflect on the meditations in the commentary on that passage. You then can meet once a week to hear God's Word together. In that group meeting, the method of holy reading would look something like this:

Listening

1. Five minutes of silence
2. Slow reading of the biblical passage for that week
3. A minute of silent meditation on the passage
4. Briefly share with the group the word or phrase that struck you

Personal Message

5. A second reading of the same passage
6. A minute of silence
7. Where does this touch your life today?
8. Responses: I hear, I see, etc.

Life Response

9. Brief silence
10. What does God want you to do today in light of this word?

Group Prayer

11. Have each member of the group pray aloud for the person on his or her left, asking God to bless the word he has given them.

The procedure suggested here can be used in churches or in neighborhood Bible studies. Church members would use the daily readings Monday to Friday in their daily devotionals. This commentary intentionally provides no readings on the sixth day so we can spend Saturdays as a time of rest—not rest from Bible study, but a time to let God's Word quietly work its way deep into our hearts. Sunday during Bible school or in-home meetings, the group would meet to experience the weekly readings together, using the group method described above. The sermon each Sunday could even be on the passage for that week.

Some churches have used this structure to great advantage. In the hallways of those church buildings, the talk is not of the local football team or the weather, but of the shared experience of the Word of God for that week.

And that is the purpose of our personal and communal study—to hear the voice of God, our loving Father, who wants us to love him in return. He deeply desires a personal relationship with us. *Father, Son, and Spirit, make a home inside us* (see John 14:16–17, 23). Our loving God speaks to his children! But we must listen for his voice. That listening is not a matter of gritting our teeth and trying harder to hear. Instead, it is part of our entire life with God. That is what Bible study is all about.

Through daily personal prayer and meditation on God's Word and through a communal reading of Scripture, our most important conversation partner, the Holy Spirit, will do his mysterious and marvelous work. Among other things, the Spirit pours God's love into our hearts (Rom. 5:5), bears witness to our spirits that we are God's children (Rom. 8:16), intercedes for us with God (Rom. 8:26), and enlightens us as to God's will (Eph. 1:17).

So this is an invitation to personal daily Bible study, to praying the Scriptures, to sharing with fellow believers, to hearing the voice of God. God will bless us, our families, our churches, and his world if we take the time to be still, listen, and do his word.

THE SPIRITUALITY OF KINGS, CHRONICLES, EZRA, NEHEMIAH, AND ESTHER

The books of 1 and 2 Kings and 1 and 2 Chronicles tell mostly the same stories from different perspectives (much like the four Gospels in the New Testament). Both pairs of books tell the stories of the kings of Israel and Judah, with particular emphasis on the line of David. Chronicles is a late telling of the stories after Judah returns from exile.

In the children's Sunday school class at our church, a banner runs around the top of the wall with the faces of the kings of Israel and Judah. The good kings are smiling. The bad kings are frowning.

What makes a good king? It's not whether he smiles or frowns. It's not his success as a warrior. It's not how much he taxes the people. Being a good king depends on one thing: Is the Lord the priority?

Does the king worship the Lord alone? Does he lead the people to worship the Lord alone? Does he destroy the idols?

Israel and Judah easily forgot that the Lord alone was their king. They went after other gods and began to put their trust in earthly kings. Some of the good kings, like Asa, Hezekiah, and Josiah, led revivals of trust in the Lord alone, restoring the proper worship of God. But when the king (or sometimes queen) followed other gods, the Lord raised up prophets, men and women who spoke from God. They invited God's people to return to him and warned of the consequences if they did not.

Prophets warned not only in word but in power. Elijah, Elisha, and others brought fire from heaven, multiplied food, healed the sick, and even raised the dead by the power of the Lord.

So these books of kings and prophets are really books about the God who rules his people as the true King and who speaks kind and frightening words to them. The spirituality of these books focuses on loyalty to that God.

The Spirituality of Ezra and Nehemiah

These two books tell the story of the return of God's people from exile. Ezra tells the story from the perspective of one who is priest and scribe. Nehemiah tells it from the perspective of a political leader.

It is God who acts through pagan human rulers to return his people to the promised land. These books are therefore books of hope. Although God's people abandoned him, he did not abandon them. After their time of punishment in exile, the Lord brought them home. Despite opposition, the walls of Jerusalem were rebuilt, the temple was restored, and the people returned to loyalty to the covenant God made with their ancestors and with them.

In addition to the spirituality of hope in these books, there is also a spirituality of separation. God reminded his people that they must be different from other nations. Ezra in particular led them to this pledge of purity, serving the Lord alone.

The Spirituality of Esther

The book of Esther seems out of place in the Bible, telling the story of a girl who becomes queen after winning a beauty pageant. It has no mention of the temple, covenants, or even God! With the surrounding books talking so much about the kings of Israel and Judah, Esther is set in a different country, Persia, at the court of a foreign king.

Even though the Lord is not mentioned in Esther, the book points to a God who is active behind the scenes. He is the Lord of all nations, although at first it may not look that way. And he works his will through his people in surprising ways. Even here, it is the Lord alone who is King.

MEDITATIONS

GOD BUILDS HIS TEMPLE

1 Chronicles 28:1–21 NLT

DAY ONE READING AND QUESTIONS

David summoned all the officials of Israel to Jerusalem—the leaders of the tribes, the commanders of the army divisions, the other generals and captains, the overseers of the royal property and livestock, the palace officials, the mighty men, and all the other brave warriors in the kingdom. David rose to his feet and said: "My brothers and my people! It was my desire to build a Temple where the Ark of the LORD's Covenant, God's footstool, could rest permanently. I made the necessary preparations for building it, but God said to me, 'You must not build a Temple to honor my name, for you are a warrior and have shed much blood.'

"Yet the LORD, the God of Israel, has chosen me from among all my father's family to be king over Israel forever. For he has chosen the tribe of Judah to rule, and from among the families of Judah he chose my father's family. And from among my father's sons the LORD was pleased to make me king over all Israel. And from among my sons—for the LORD has given me many—he chose Solomon to succeed me on the throne of Israel and to rule over the LORD's kingdom. He said to me, 'Your son Solomon will build my Temple and its courtyards, for I have chosen him as my son, and I will be his father. And if he continues to obey my commands and regulations as he does now, I will make his kingdom last forever.'"

1. *What does it mean that the ark of the covenant is the Lord's footstool?*

2. *Why would God not allow David to build the temple? Was David not a warrior for the Lord?*

3. *How is the Lord a Father to Solomon? Isn't he a Father to everyone?*

DAY TWO READING AND QUESTIONS

"So now, with God as our witness, and in the sight of all Israel—the LORD's assembly—I give you this charge. Be careful to obey all the commands of the LORD your God, so that you may continue to possess this good land and leave it to your children as a permanent inheritance.

"And Solomon, my son, learn to know the God of your ancestors intimately. Worship and serve him with your whole heart and a willing mind. For the LORD sees every heart and knows every plan and thought. If you seek him, you will find him. But if you forsake him, he will reject you forever. So take this seriously. The LORD has chosen you to build a Temple as his sanctuary. Be strong, and do the work."

Then David gave Solomon the plans for the Temple and its surroundings, including the entry room, the storerooms, the upstairs rooms, the inner rooms, and the inner sanctuary—which was the place of atonement. David also gave Solomon all the plans he had in mind for the courtyards of the LORD's Temple, the outside rooms, the treasuries, and the rooms for the gifts dedicated to the LORD. The king also gave Solomon the instructions concerning the work of the various divisions of priests and Levites in the Temple of the LORD. And he gave specifications for the items in the Temple that were to be used for worship.

1. *Why does David charge the leaders of Israel to obey the commands of the Lord?*

2. *Why is it important that the Lord knows the heart of Solomon?*

3. *Who made the plans for the Temple?*

DAY THREE READING AND QUESTIONS

David gave instructions regarding how much gold and silver should be used to make the items needed for service. He told Solomon the amount of gold needed for the gold lampstands and lamps, and the amount of silver for the silver lampstands and lamps, depending on how each would be used. He designated the amount of gold for the table on which the Bread of the Presence would be placed and the amount of silver for other tables.

David also designated the amount of gold for the solid gold meat hooks used to handle the sacrificial meat and for the basins, pitchers, and dishes, as well as the amount of silver for every dish. He designated the amount of refined gold for the altar of incense. Finally, he gave him a plan for the LORD's "chariot"—the gold cherubim whose wings were stretched out over the Ark of the LORD's Covenant. "Every part of this plan," David told Solomon, "was given to me in writing from the hand of the LORD."

1. *Why were gold and silver used for the Temple furnishings?*

2. *Why are the cherubim on the top of the ark called "the Lord's chariot"? What were chariots used for?*

3. *Why is it significant that the plans for the Temple came directly from the Lord?*

DAY FOUR READING AND QUESTIONS

Then David continued, "Be strong and courageous, and do the work. Don't be afraid or discouraged, for the LORD God, my God, is with you. He will not fail you or forsake you. He will see to it that all the work related to the Temple of the LORD is finished correctly. The various divisions of priests and Levites will serve in the Temple of God. Others with skills of every kind will volunteer, and the officials and the entire nation are at your command."

1. *Why does David urge Solomon to be strong and courageous?*

2. *Why might Solomon be afraid to build the temple?*

3. *Who will help Solomon build the temple?*

DAY FIVE READING AND QUESTIONS

Go back and read 1 Chronicles 28:1–21.

1. *Who is the real builder of the temple?*

2. *What was the purpose of the temple?*

3. *Why waste silver and gold on the temple furnishings when that money could be used to help the poor?*

Meditation on 1 Chronicles 28:1–21

The temple was a long time coming.

Back in the time of Moses, the Lord had Israel build a tabernacle, a movable sanctuary. He gave them plans for the furniture, including the ark of the covenant. On top of the ark were two heavenly beings with outstretched wings, looking much like the thrones of ancient kingdoms. This was the throne of God. This was the chariot the Lord would ride to protect his people in battle.

But Israel foolishly lost the ark to the Philistines (1 Sam. 5). There were several failed attempts to bring it back to Israel. When David conquered Jerusalem and made it his capital, he brought the ark there (after another failed attempt). Finally, many years after Moses, the ark was where it should be, in Jerusalem, but there was no permanent home for it.

Until David. He so much wanted to build a temple for the Lord. He made all the preparations. But the Lord would not let him.

Why not? The Lord told him, "You must not build a Temple to honor my name, for you are a warrior and have shed much blood."

But did David not fight for the Lord? Did he not defend the Lord's people? How can the Lord fault David for fighting when the ark itself has the Lord's chariot (a weapon of war) on top?

Perhaps that is the point. The Lord is the one, the only one, who gives victory in battle. David usually knew that. But if David built the temple, God's people might have thought the temple was all about the triumphs of David—not about the Lord.

When building a great building or organization or church, it is tempting to think we are doing great things for God. Instead, it is the Lord who builds his temple.

"Almighty God, may we always give you the glory."

GOD GIVES WISDOM

1 Kings 3:1–28 NIV

DAY ONE READING AND QUESTIONS

Solomon made an alliance with Pharaoh king of Egypt and married his daughter. He brought her to the City of David until he finished building his palace and the temple of the LORD, and the wall around Jerusalem. The people, however, were still sacrificing at the high places, because a temple had not yet been built for the Name of the LORD. Solomon showed his love for the LORD by walking according to the instructions given him by his father David, except that he offered sacrifices and burned incense on the high places.

The king went to Gibeon to offer sacrifices, for that was the most important high place, and Solomon offered a thousand burnt offerings on that altar. At Gibeon the LORD appeared to Solomon during the night in a dream, and God said, "Ask for whatever you want me to give you."

Solomon answered, "You have shown great kindness to your servant, my father David, because he was faithful to you and righteous and upright in heart. You have continued this great kindness to him and have given him a son to sit on his throne this very day.

"Now, LORD my God, you have made your servant king in place of my father David. But I am only a little child and do not know how to carry out my duties. Your servant is here among the people you have chosen, a great people, too numerous to count or number. So give your servant a discerning heart to govern your people and to distinguish between right and wrong. For who is able to govern this great people of yours?"

1. *How did Solomon make an alliance with Egypt? What does this tell us about his power?*

2. *Solomon offers a thousand sacrifices. What does this tell us about his relationship with the Lord?*

3. *Solomon asks the Lord for a discerning heart. What does this tell us about Solomon?*

DAY TWO READING AND QUESTIONS

The LORD was pleased that Solomon had asked for this. So God said to him, "Since you have asked for this and not for long life or wealth for yourself, nor have asked for the death of your enemies but for discernment in administering justice, I will do what you have asked. I will give you a wise and discerning heart, so that there will never have been anyone like you, nor will there ever be. Moreover, I will give you what you have not asked for—both wealth and honor—so that in your lifetime you will have no equal among kings. And if you walk in obedience to me and keep my decrees and commands as David your father did, I will give you a long life." Then Solomon awoke—and he realized it had been a dream.

He returned to Jerusalem, stood before the ark of the LORD's covenant and sacrificed burnt offerings and fellowship offerings. Then he gave a feast for all his court.

1. *Why is the Lord pleased with Solomon's request?*

2. *Why does the Lord add the gifts of wealth and honor to Solomon?*

3. *Why is it significant that Solomon sacrifices before the ark of the covenant?*

DAY THREE READING AND QUESTIONS

Now two prostitutes came to the king and stood before him. One of them said, "Pardon me, my lord. This woman and I live in the same house, and I had a baby while she was there with me. The third day after my child was born, this woman also had a baby. We were alone; there was no one in the house but the two of us.

"During the night this woman's son died because she lay on him. So she got up in the middle of the night and took my son from my side while I your servant was asleep. She put him by her breast and put her dead son by my breast. The next morning, I got up to nurse my son—and he was dead! But when I looked at him closely in the morning light, I saw that it wasn't the son I had borne."

The other woman said, "No! The living one is my son; the dead one is yours."

But the first one insisted, "No! The dead one is yours; the living one is mine." And so they argued before the king.

1. *What factors make this a hard case to judge?*

2. *Is one of these women responsible for the death of her son?*

3. *What is worse, accidentally killing your child or stealing the child of another?*

DAY FOUR READING AND QUESTIONS

The king said, "This one says, 'My son is alive and your son is dead,' while that one says, 'No! Your son is dead and mine is alive.'"

Then the king said, "Bring me a sword." So they brought a sword for the king. He then gave an order: "Cut the living child in two and give half to one and half to the other."

The woman whose son was alive was deeply moved out of love for her son and said to the king, "Please, my LORD, give her the living baby! Don't kill him!"

But the other said, "Neither I nor you shall have him. Cut him in two!"

Then the king gave his ruling: "Give the living baby to the first woman. Do not kill him; she is his mother."

When all Israel heard the verdict the king had given, they held the king in awe, because they saw that he had wisdom from God to administer justice.

1. *Would Solomon have actually cut the child in two?*

2. *What kind of woman would agree to having the child cut in two? What had this woman done?*

3. *Why is the woman who lied and killed her own son not punished?*

DAY FIVE READING AND QUESTIONS

Go back and read 1 Kings 3:1–28.

1. *Solomon asks for a discerning heart. The people say he received wisdom from God. What is the relationship between discernment and wisdom?*

2. *Kings acted as judges in Israel. Which is harder, being a king or a judge? Which requires more wisdom?*

3. *Why do the people hold Solomon in awe? How is the word "awe" usually used in the Bible?*

Meditation on 1 Kings 3:1–28

"Hard cases make bad law." This is an axiom of the justice system. It means laws should generally cover ordinary circumstances, not extreme ones.

Solomon faced a hard case, perhaps the hardest. It was a "she said" versus "she said" case with no witnesses except the two plaintiffs. How can one decide? By questioning the women? That doesn't help. Unlike today, there was no forensic evidence.

So Solomon got his sword and gave orders for the child to be cut in two. I remember as a child how shocked I was hearing this story for the first time. How could the Lord's anointed king cut an innocent infant in half?

But it worked. The real mother would do anything, even give her child away, to preserve his life. Solomon was smarter than the greatest detective in mystery novels or on television.

And that's the point. The smarts (discernment or wisdom) Solomon had were not his own. They came directly from the Lord. They were God's gift. The Lord, not Solomon, rules his people. The Lord, not Solomon, brings justice. The proverbial wisdom of Solomon was the wisdom of God.

We too, as God's people, can pray for his gifts. But the gifts he gives are not just for us but for all his people. The Lord reigns.

"Lord of generosity, may we rejoice in our blessings because you bless others through us."

GOD LISTENS TO HIS PEOPLE

1 Kings 8:22–53 ESV

DAY ONE READING AND QUESTIONS

Then Solomon stood before the altar of the LORD in the presence of all the assembly of Israel and spread out his hands toward heaven, and said, "O LORD, God of Israel, there is no God like you, in heaven above or on earth beneath, keeping covenant and showing steadfast love to your servants who walk before you with all their heart; you have kept with your servant David my father what you declared to him. You spoke with your mouth, and with your hand have fulfilled it this day. Now therefore, O LORD, God of Israel, keep for your servant David my father what you have promised him, saying, 'You shall not lack a man to sit before me on the throne of Israel, if only your sons pay close attention to their way, to walk before me as you have walked before me.' Now therefore, O God of Israel, let your word be confirmed, which you have spoken to your servant David my father.

"But will God indeed dwell on the earth? Behold, heaven and the highest heaven cannot contain you; how much less this house that I have built! Yet have regard to the prayer of your servant and to his plea, O LORD my God, listening to the cry and to the prayer that your servant prays before you this day, that your eyes may be open night and day toward this house, the place of which you have said, 'My name shall be there,' that you may listen to the prayer that your servant offers toward this place. And listen to the plea of your servant and of your people Israel, when they pray toward this place. And listen in heaven your dwelling place, and when you hear, forgive."

1. *How does Solomon describe the Lord in this prayer?*

2. *Why is it important that Israel knows the temple will not contain God?*

3. *What does Solomon want to happen at the temple?*

DAY TWO READING AND QUESTIONS

"If a man sins against his neighbor and is made to take an oath and comes and swears his oath before your altar in this house, then hear in heaven and act and judge your servants, condemning the guilty by bringing his conduct on his own head, and vindicating the righteous by rewarding him according to his righteousness.

"When your people Israel are defeated before the enemy because they have sinned against you, and if they turn again to you and acknowledge your name and pray and plead with you in this house, then hear in heaven and forgive the sin of your people Israel and bring them again to the land that you gave to their fathers.

"When heaven is shut up and there is no rain because they have sinned against you, if they pray toward this place and acknowledge your name and turn from their sin, when you afflict them, then hear in heaven and forgive the sin of your servants, your people Israel, when you teach them the good way in which they should walk, and grant rain upon your land, which you have given to your people as an inheritance.

"If there is famine in the land, if there is pestilence or blight or mildew or locust or caterpillar, if their enemy besieges them in the land at their gates, whatever plague, whatever sickness there is, whatever prayer, whatever plea is made by any man or by all your people Israel, each knowing the affliction of his own heart and stretching out his hands toward this house, then hear in heaven your dwelling place and forgive and act and render to each whose heart you know, according to all his ways (for you, you only, know the hearts of all the children of mankind), that they may fear you all the days that they live in the land that you gave to our fathers."

1. *Besides hearing prayer, what else does Solomon ask the Lord to do at the temple?*

2. *Why might the calamities listed in these verses fall upon Israel?*

3. *What is the picture of God in these verses?*

DAY THREE READING AND QUESTIONS

"Likewise, when a foreigner, who is not of your people Israel, comes from a far country for your name's sake (for they shall hear of your great name and your mighty hand, and of your outstretched arm), when he comes and prays toward this house, hear in heaven your dwelling place and do according to all for which the foreigner calls to you, in order that all the peoples of the earth may know your name and fear you, as do your people Israel, and that they may know that this house that I have built is called by your name.

"If your people go out to battle against their enemy, by whatever way you shall send them, and they pray to the Lord toward the city that you have chosen and the house that I have built for your name, then hear in heaven their prayer and their plea, and maintain their cause.

"If they sin against you—for there is no one who does not sin—and you are angry with them and give them to an enemy, so that they are carried away captive to the land of the enemy, far off or near, yet if they turn their heart in the land to which they have been carried captive, and repent and plead with you in the land of their captors, saying, 'We have sinned and have acted perversely and wickedly,' if they repent with all their heart and with all their soul in the land of their enemies, who carried them captive, and pray to you toward their land, which you gave to their fathers, the city that you have chosen, and the house that I have built for your name, then hear in heaven your dwelling place their prayer and their plea, and maintain their cause . . ."

1. *Is it surprising that the temple is a place for foreigners? Why or why not?*

2. *Is it surprising that exile is mentioned here? Why or why not?*

3. *Does one have to be at the temple to have prayer heard by the Lord?*

DAY FOUR READING AND QUESTIONS

". . . and forgive your people who have sinned against you, and all their transgressions that they have committed against you, and grant them compassion in the sight of those who carried them captive, that they may have compassion on them (for they are

> your people, and your heritage, which you brought out of Egypt, from the midst of the iron furnace). Let your eyes be open to the plea of your servant and to the plea of your people Israel, giving ear to them whenever they call to you. For you separated them from among all the peoples of the earth to be your heritage, as you declared through Moses your servant, when you brought our fathers out of Egypt, O Lord God."

1. *Why would the Lord forgive Israel?*

2. *Why is the Exodus from Egypt mentioned here?*

3. *How is Israel a "separated" people?*

DAY FIVE READING AND QUESTIONS

Go back and read 1 Kings 8:22–53.

1. *Does the Lord dwell in the temple?*

2. *If the temple does not contain the Lord, why did God tell Solomon to build it?*

3. *Why do you think there is no mention of sacrifices at the temple in these verses?*

Meditation on 1 Kings 8:22–53

Humans live in a place, whether alone or with others. That place becomes important to us. We might at first call it a house, but soon we call it home.

God is everywhere. No place can contain him. No place is God's home. Or (maybe better) every place is God's home.

David wanted to build a house for God. The Lord reminded him that he did not ask for or need a house (see 1 Chron. 17:1–6). Yet God tells Solomon to build the temple.

Why? God does not need a temple to show his glory. The whole world shows his glory! But God agrees for his glory to fill the temple for the sake of his people. People need a place—not to contain God but so they can approach God.

What does the Lord do in his temple? In this prayer, Solomon asks God to do one thing: to listen. And the Lord listens. He hears and forgives and heals and saves. He even listens to those outside Israel.

Later Jesus will remind God's people that the temple is to be a place of prayer for all nations (Matt. 21:13, quoting Isa. 56:7). Jesus himself is God's temple, the place where the Lord listens to his people.

"Lord of the temple, thank you for the temple named Jesus. Thank you for hearing us."

GOD MEANS WHAT HE SAYS

1 Kings 13:1–34 NLT

DAY ONE READING AND QUESTIONS

At the LORD's command, a man of God from Judah went to Bethel, arriving there just as Jeroboam was approaching the altar to burn incense. Then at the LORD's command, he shouted, "O altar, altar! This is what the LORD says: A child named Josiah will be born into the dynasty of David. On you he will sacrifice the priests from the pagan shrines who come here to burn incense, and human bones will be burned on you." That same day the man of God gave a sign to prove his message. He said, "The LORD has promised to give this sign: This altar will split apart, and its ashes will be poured out on the ground."

When King Jeroboam heard the man of God speaking against the altar at Bethel, he pointed at him and shouted, "Seize that man!" But instantly the king's hand became paralyzed in that position, and he couldn't pull it back. At the same time a wide crack appeared in the altar, and the ashes poured out, just as the man of God had predicted in his message from the LORD.

The king cried out to the man of God, "Please ask the LORD your God to restore my hand again!" So the man of God prayed to the LORD, and the king's hand was restored and he could move it again.

1. *When Solomon built the temple, the Lord intended that all sacrifices should be offered there. Why would Jeroboam offer a sacrifice elsewhere? To what god was Jeroboam making his sacrifice?*

2. *What did Jeroboam want to do to the prophet? Why?*

3. *Why does the Lord restore Jeroboam's hand?*

DAY TWO READING AND QUESTIONS

Then the king said to the man of God, "Come to the palace with me and have something to eat, and I will give you a gift."

But the man of God said to the king, "Even if you gave me half of everything you own, I would not go with you. I would not eat or drink anything in this place. For the LORD gave me this command: 'You must not eat or drink anything while you are there, and do not return to Judah by the same way you came.'" So he left Bethel and went home another way.

As it happened, there was an old prophet living in Bethel, and his sons came home and told him what the man of God had done in Bethel that day. They also told their father what the man had said to the king. The old prophet asked them, "Which way did he go?" So they showed their father which road the man of God had taken. "Quick, saddle the donkey," the old man said. So they saddled the donkey for him, and he mounted it.

Then he rode after the man of God and found him sitting under a great tree. The old prophet asked him, "Are you the man of God who came from Judah?"

"Yes, I am," he replied.

Then he said to the man of God, "Come home with me and eat some food."

"No, I cannot," he replied. "I am not allowed to eat or drink anything here in this place. For the LORD gave me this command: 'You must not eat or drink anything while you are there, and do not return to Judah by the same way you came.'"

1. *Why did Jeroboam invite the man of God to eat with him?*

2. *Why do you think the Lord told the prophet not to eat or drink at Bethel?*

3. *Why did the old prophet pursue the young one?*

DAY THREE READING AND QUESTIONS

But the old prophet answered, "I am a prophet, too, just as you are. And an angel gave me this command from the LORD: 'Bring him home with you so he can have something to eat and drink.'" But the old man was lying to him. So they went back together, and the man of God ate and drank at the prophet's home.

Then while they were sitting at the table, a command from the LORD came to the old prophet. He cried out to the man of God from Judah, "This is what the LORD says: You have defied the word of the LORD and have disobeyed the command the LORD your God gave you. You came back to this place and ate and drank where he told you not to eat or drink. Because of this, your body will not be buried in the grave of your ancestors."

After the man of God had finished eating and drinking, the old prophet saddled his own donkey for him, and the man of God started off again. But as he was traveling along, a lion came out and killed him. His body lay there on the road, with the donkey and the lion standing beside it. People who passed by saw the body lying in the road and the lion standing beside it, and they went and reported it in Bethel, where the old prophet lived.

When the prophet heard the report, he said, "It is the man of God who disobeyed the LORD's command. The LORD has fulfilled his word by causing the lion to attack and kill him."

1. *Why would the old prophet lie to the prophet from Judah?*

2. *Why would the Lord kill the prophet from Judah when he was the victim of a lie?*

3. *Why is it significant that the old prophet lived in Bethel?*

DAY FOUR READING AND QUESTIONS

Then the prophet said to his sons, "Saddle a donkey for me." So they saddled a donkey, and he went out and found the body lying in the road. The donkey and lion were still standing there beside it, for the lion had not eaten the body nor attacked the donkey. So the prophet laid the body of the man of God on the donkey and took it back to the town to mourn over him and bury him. He laid the body in his own grave, crying out in grief, "Oh, my brother!"

Afterward the prophet said to his sons, "When I die, bury me in the grave where the man of God is buried. Lay my bones beside his bones. For the message the LORD told him to proclaim against the altar in Bethel and against the pagan shrines in the towns of Samaria will certainly come true."

But even after this, Jeroboam did not turn from his evil ways. He continued to choose priests from the common people. He appointed anyone who wanted to become a priest for the pagan shrines. This became a great sin and resulted in the utter destruction of Jeroboam's dynasty from the face of the earth.

1. *Why does the old prophet mourn over the body of the man of God? Is his mourning sincere?*

2. *How does the old prophet know that the prophecy against the altar at Bethel will come true?*

3. *Why does Jeroboam not turn from his ways after such a dramatic sign from the man of God?*

DAY FIVE READING AND QUESTIONS

Go back and read 1 Kings 13:1–34.

1. *Was the old prophet a genuine prophet of the Lord?*

2. *Should the man of God from Judah have doubted the word of the old prophet?*

3. *How can you tell a true prophet from a false one?*

Meditation on 1 Kings 13:1–34

I don't know what to make of the old prophet in this story.

Is he a false prophet, aligned with the pagan-worshiping Jeroboam? If so, he lies to the man of God to intentionally get the man in trouble with the Lord.

But if that is so, why does he go to the trouble of finding the man's body and burying it in his own tomb?

Or is he a true prophet? If so, perhaps he's thrilled to see another prophet of the Lord in Jeroboam's territory. He wants so much to have fellowship with him that he makes up a story about an angelic message.

Lies have consequences, whether they are intentionally meant to harm or they spring from what the liar thinks is a good motive.

What do we make of the Lord in this story? Shouldn't the Lord have forgiven the man of God since he was deceived? Should the Lord not have punished the old prophet instead?

This story is about the trustworthiness of God. When the Lord tells the man of God not to eat in Bethel, he means it. Disobedience brings severe consequences, whatever the circumstances of that disobedience. And when the Lord tells King Jeroboam not to worship pagan gods at Bethel, he means it. Disobedience brings severe consequences. And when the Lord tells us, his people, to worship him alone, he means it.

"Our Lord, give us the wisdom and strength to hear your voice alone. Save us from voices that deceive us."

GOD'S PEOPLE SEEK HIM

2 Chronicles 14:1–6; 15:1–19 NIV

DAY ONE READING AND QUESTIONS

And Abijah rested with his ancestors and was buried in the City of David. Asa his son succeeded him as king, and in his days the country was at peace for ten years.

Asa did what was good and right in the eyes of the LORD his God. He removed the foreign altars and the high places, smashed the sacred stones and cut down the Asherah poles. He commanded Judah to seek the LORD, the God of their ancestors, and to obey his laws and commands. He removed the high places and incense altars in every town in Judah, and the kingdom was at peace under him. He built up the fortified cities of Judah, since the land was at peace. No one was at war with him during those years, for the LORD gave him rest.

1. *What makes one a "good" king in Judah?*

2. *What are the consequences of seeking the Lord?*

3. *What was the cause of rest and peace under Asa?*

DAY TWO READING AND QUESTIONS

The Spirit of God came on Azariah son of Oded. He went out to meet Asa and said to him, "Listen to me, Asa and all Judah and Benjamin. The LORD is with you when you are with him. If you seek him, he will be found by you, but if you forsake him, he will forsake you. For a long time Israel was without the true God, without a priest to teach and without the law. But in their distress they turned to the LORD, the God of Israel, and sought him, and he was found by them. In those days it was not safe to travel about, for all the inhabitants of the lands were in great turmoil. One nation was being crushed by another and one city by another, because God was troubling them with every kind of distress. But as for you, be strong and do not give up, for your work will be rewarded."

1. *Why does the Lord send the prophet Azariah to Asa?*

2. *What is the role of the Spirit in this passage?*

3. *What is the picture of the Lord God in these verses?*

DAY THREE READING AND QUESTIONS

When Asa heard these words and the prophecy of Azariah son of Oded the prophet, he took courage. He removed the detestable idols from the whole land of Judah and Benjamin and from the towns he had captured in the hills of Ephraim. He repaired the altar of the LORD that was in front of the portico of the LORD's temple.

Then he assembled all Judah and Benjamin and the people from Ephraim, Manasseh and Simeon who had settled among them, for large numbers had come over to him from Israel when they saw that the LORD his God was with him.

They assembled at Jerusalem in the third month of the fifteenth year of Asa's reign. At that time they sacrificed to the LORD seven hundred head of cattle and seven thousand sheep and goats from the plunder they had brought back. They entered into a covenant to seek the LORD, the God of their ancestors, with all their heart and soul. All who would not seek the LORD, the God of Israel, were to be put to death, whether small or great, man or woman. They took an oath to the LORD with loud acclamation, with shouting and with trumpets and horns. All Judah rejoiced about the oath because they had sworn it wholeheartedly. They sought God eagerly, and he was found by them. So the LORD gave them rest on every side.

1. *How did Asa react to the prophet's message?*

2. *What does it mean to enter a covenant to seek the Lord?*

3. *How does taking an oath relate to the covenant?*

DAY FOUR READING AND QUESTIONS

King Asa also deposed his grandmother Maakah from her position as queen mother, because she had made a repulsive image for the worship of Asherah. Asa cut it down, broke it up and burned it in the Kidron Valley. Although he did not remove the high places from Israel, Asa's heart was fully committed to the LORD all his life. He brought into the temple of God the silver and gold and the articles that he and his father had dedicated.

There was no more war until the thirty-fifth year of Asa's reign.

1. *Asa deposes his own grandmother. What does that tell you about Asa?*

2. *Why did Asa not remove all the high places where pagan gods were worshiped?*

3. *Why is it important that Asa brought silver and gold into the temple?*

DAY FIVE READING AND QUESTIONS

Go back and read 2 Chronicles 14:1–6; 15:1–19.

1. *Do we have a covenant with the Lord? If so, when did he make that covenant with us?*

2. *Should we take oaths to the Lord? If so, what does that look like?*

3. *Why is idolatry such a problem for God's people?*

Meditation on 2 Chronicles 14:1–6; 15:1–19

Asa is a good king. But it's hard to be a good king because there are powerful people who worship other gods, even Asa's grandmother! Asa needs strength from the Lord to stand against the idols of his day. And the Spirit provides that strength by sending the prophet Azariah to Asa.

With that encouragement, Asa leads a revival of worship to the Lord. The people renew their covenant with God. They take oaths to follow him alone. They destroy some (but not all) of the places of idol worship. And this is not just an outward obedience. "All Judah rejoiced about the oath because they had sworn it wholeheartedly. They sought God eagerly, and he was found by them."

The Lord has made a covenant with us. At the Last Supper, Jesus says, "This cup is the new covenant in my blood, which is poured out for you" (Luke 22:20 NIV). We made an oath to follow Jesus alone at our baptisms. We did it wholeheartedly. But we also must cast the idols of our age away from us.

The places of idol worship in our day are harder to see, but they are there. Like Judah, we easily fall into serving idols alongside serving the Lord. Like them, as God's people we must hear the words of Azariah: "The LORD is with you when you are with him. If you seek him, he will be found by you, but if you forsake him, he will forsake you."

"God of the covenant, may we each day commit ourselves with all our heart to worship you alone."

GOD RAISES THE DEAD

1 Kings 17:1–24 ESV

DAY ONE READING AND QUESTIONS

Now Elijah the Tishbite, of Tishbe in Gilead, said to Ahab, "As the LORD, the God of Israel, lives, before whom I stand, there shall be neither dew nor rain these years, except by my word." And the word of the LORD came to him: "Depart from here and turn eastward and hide yourself by the brook Cherith, which is east of the Jordan. You shall drink from the brook, and I have commanded the ravens to feed you there." So he went and did according to the word of the LORD. He went and lived by the brook Cherith that is east of the Jordan. And the ravens brought him bread and meat in the morning, and bread and meat in the evening, and he drank from the brook. And after a while the brook dried up, because there was no rain in the land.

1. *Why does the Lord send a drought?*

2. *What other Bible story do you think of when you read of the ravens feeding Elisha?*

3. *How does the Lord provide water for his people in the Bible?*

DAY TWO READING AND QUESTIONS

Then the word of the LORD came to him, "Arise, go to Zarephath, which belongs to Sidon, and dwell there. Behold, I have commanded a widow there to feed you." So he arose and went to Zarephath. And when he came to the gate of the city, behold, a widow was there gathering sticks. And he called to her and said, "Bring me a little water in a vessel, that I may drink." And as she was going to bring it, he called to her and said, "Bring me a morsel of bread in your hand." And she said, "As the LORD your God lives, I have nothing baked, only a handful of flour in a jar and a little oil in a jug. And now I am gathering a couple of sticks that I may go in and prepare it for myself and my son, that we may eat it and die." And Elijah said to her, "Do not fear; go and do as you have said. But first make me a little cake of it and bring it to me, and afterward make something for yourself and your son. For thus says the LORD, the God of Israel, 'The jar of flour shall not be spent, and the jug of oil shall not be empty, until the day that the LORD sends rain upon the earth.'" And she went and did as Elijah said. And she and he and her household ate for many days. The jar of flour was not spent, neither did the jug of oil become empty, according to the word of the LORD that he spoke by Elijah.

1. *How are widows often described in the Bible? How desperate is this widow?*

2. *How did the woman know she was to feed Elijah?*

3. *What other biblical miracle does this remind you of?*

DAY THREE READING AND QUESTIONS

After this the son of the woman, the mistress of the house, became ill. And his illness was so severe that there was no breath left in him. And she said to Elijah, "What have you against me, O man of God? You have come to me to bring my sin to remembrance and to cause the death of my son!" And he said to her, "Give me your son." And he took him from her arms and carried him up into the upper chamber where he lodged, and laid him on his own bed. And he cried to the LORD, "O LORD my God, have you brought calamity even upon the widow with whom I sojourn, by killing her son?"

1. *Whom does the woman blame for her son's illness?*

2. *Why does the woman say Elijah brought her sin to remembrance?*

3. *Whom does Elijah blame for the son's illness?*

DAY FOUR READING AND QUESTIONS

Then he stretched himself upon the child three times and cried to the LORD, "O LORD my God, let this child's life come into him again." And the LORD listened to the voice of Elijah. And the life of the child came into him again, and he revived. And Elijah took the child and brought him down from the upper chamber into the house and delivered him to his mother. And Elijah said, "See, your son lives." And the woman said to Elijah, "Now I know that you are a man of God, and that the word of the LORD in your mouth is truth."

1. *Why does Elijah stretch himself over the child three times?*

2. *Why does the Lord hear Elijah's prayer?*

3. *Why does the woman believe Elijah speaks the word of the Lord?*

DAY FIVE READING AND QUESTIONS

Go back and read 1 Kings 17:1–24.

1. *This widow is not an Israelite. How does that change how we read these stories?*

2. *How does the relationship between the widow and Elijah change as the story unfolds?*

3. *What is the relationship between being a miracle worker and speaking the word of the Lord?*

Meditation on 1 Kings 17:1–24

Is it good to have a prophet in your house?

This widow is not sure. After all, she is not from Israel, so this prophet speaks of a strange God. He also is a demanding prophet, asking that she feed him when there's not enough food for her and her son.

But then a miracle happens! The flour and oil do not run out. This man must indeed be a prophet of the true God.

Then her son falls deathly ill. What could cause this? What has changed in her life? Only the visit of this prophet. He and his God must have caused this. She knew her sins would find her out, and now this prophet has brought retribution not on her but on her son.

But the prophet prays to his God and the son is brought back to life. The widow says to Elijah, "Now I know that you are a man of God, and that the word of the LORD in your mouth is truth."

Are we not like this woman? Even as God's people, we tend to trust the Lord when he blesses and blame the Lord when trouble comes. We trust the word of the Lord when it's a word we want to hear.

Is it a good thing to have a prophet in your house? Yes! But it is not an easy thing. Is it a good thing to have the Lord in your house? Yes! But it is not an easy thing.

"God of life, may we trust you at all times, good and bad."

GOD ANSWERS PRAYER

1 Kings 18:15–40 NLT

DAY ONE READING AND QUESTIONS

But Elijah said, "I swear by the LORD Almighty, in whose presence I stand, that I will present myself to Ahab this very day."

So Obadiah went to tell Ahab that Elijah had come, and Ahab went out to meet Elijah. When Ahab saw him, he exclaimed, "So, is it really you, you troublemaker of Israel?"

"I have made no trouble for Israel," Elijah replied. "You and your family are the troublemakers, for you have refused to obey the commands of the LORD and have worshiped the images of Baal instead. Now summon all Israel to join me at Mount Carmel, along with the 450 prophets of Baal and the 400 prophets of Asherah who are supported by Jezebel."

So Ahab summoned all the people of Israel and the prophets to Mount Carmel. Then Elijah stood in front of them and said, "How much longer will you waver, hobbling between two opinions? If the LORD is God, follow him! But if Baal is God, then follow him!" But the people were completely silent.

1. *Why does Ahab call Elijah a troublemaker?*

2. *Why does Elijah call Ahab a troublemaker?*

3. *Why does Elijah say Israel is hobbling between two opinions? About what could they not make up their minds?*

DAY TWO READING AND QUESTIONS

Then Elijah said to them, "I am the only prophet of the LORD who is left, but Baal has 450 prophets. Now bring two bulls. The prophets of Baal may choose whichever one they wish and cut it into pieces and lay it on the wood of their altar, but without setting fire to it. I will prepare the other bull and lay it on the wood on the altar, but not set fire to it. Then call on the name of your god, and I will call on the name of the LORD. The god who answers by setting fire to the wood is the true God!" And all the people agreed.

Then Elijah said to the prophets of Baal, "You go first, for there are many of you. Choose one of the bulls, and prepare it and call on the name of your god. But do not set fire to the wood."

So they prepared one of the bulls and placed it on the altar. Then they called on the name of Baal from morning until noontime, shouting, "O Baal, answer us!" But there was no reply of any kind. Then they danced, hobbling around the altar they had made.

About noontime Elijah began mocking them. "You'll have to shout louder," he scoffed, "for surely he is a god! Perhaps he is daydreaming, or is relieving himself. Or maybe he is away on a trip, or is asleep and needs to be wakened!"

So they shouted louder, and following their normal custom, they cut themselves with knives and swords until the blood gushed out. They raved all afternoon until the time of the evening sacrifice, but still there was no sound, no reply, no response.

1. *What seems to be more popular in Israel, worship of Baal or worship of the Lord?*

2. *Why do you think Elijah let the prophets of Baal go first?*

3. *Why do the prophets of Baal have to shout loudly?*

DAY THREE READING AND QUESTIONS

Then Elijah called to the people, "Come over here!" They all crowded around him as he repaired the altar of the LORD that had been torn down. He took twelve stones, one to represent each of the tribes of Israel, and he used the stones to rebuild the altar in the name of the LORD. Then he dug a trench around the altar large enough to hold about three gallons. He piled wood on the altar, cut the bull into pieces, and laid the pieces on the wood.

Then he said, "Fill four large jars with water, and pour the water over the offering and the wood."

After they had done this, he said, "Do the same thing again!" And when they were finished, he said, "Now do it a third time!" So they did as he said, and the water ran around the altar and even filled the trench.

1. *Why is it significant that the altar to the Lord had been torn down?*

2. *Why is it significant that Elijah used twelve stones to rebuild the altar?*

3. *Why does Elijah have the prophets of Baal pour water on the offering and the wood?*

DAY FOUR READING AND QUESTIONS

At the usual time for offering the evening sacrifice, Elijah the prophet walked up to the altar and prayed, "O LORD, God of Abraham, Isaac, and Jacob, prove today that you are God in Israel and that I am your servant. Prove that I have done all this at your command. O LORD, answer me! Answer me so these people will know that you, O LORD, are God and that you have brought them back to yourself."

Immediately the fire of the LORD flashed down from heaven and burned up the young bull, the wood, the stones, and the dust. It even licked up all the water in the trench! And when all the people saw it, they fell face down on the ground and cried out, "The LORD—he is God! Yes, the LORD is God!"

Then Elijah commanded, "Seize all the prophets of Baal. Don't let a single one escape!" So the people seized them all, and Elijah took them down to the Kishon Valley and killed them there.

1. *How does Elijah's approach to the Lord contrast with the prophets' approach to Baal?*

2. *The people had forsaken the Lord. What word of hope does Elijah give them?*

3. *Elijah does not pray for fire. What does he pray for?*

DAY FIVE READING AND QUESTIONS

Go back and read 1 Kings 18:15–40.

1. *Why do the people want to serve the Lord and Baal?*

2. *Why does Baal not answer his prophets?*

3. *Why does the Lord answer Elijah?*

Meditation on 1 Kings 18:15–40

To whom did Israel pray?

They prayed to the Lord and to Baal (at least at the beginning of this story). Why? They thought the Lord was a great God to have in battle, so in times of war they prayed to him. But Baal was the god of good crops, so they also prayed to him. They hedged their bets, wavering between both.

To whom do we pray? To God alone. After all, there is only one God.

Oh yeah? Don't we also "pray" to other gods? We don't use the language of prayer, but we plead for science to give us health and good crops. We plead for the strong military to protect us in war. And we plead for a good economy to bless us all. "That's just the way the world works," we say. So we do not stop praying to the Lord, but we depend on other "gods" to make us full and well and safe and happy.

How did the prophets of Baal pray? They made a whole lot of noise! They prayed for a long time. They even cut themselves to impress their god.

How do we pray to the Lord? There's nothing wrong with lots of people praying together. Nothing wrong with shouting in prayer. Nothing wrong with long prayers. But do we sometimes think the Lord measures prayers by the number who pray or how long we pray or how loud we pray? Do we sometimes think we have to tell God exactly how to heal and bless those for whom we pray?

Elijah prays briefly. He prays alone. He prays in faith. He trusts the Lord will keep the promises God made to Abraham, Isaac, and Jacob. He trusts that, even now, after his people had abandoned their exclusive covenant with the Lord, that God will bring them back to him.

To whom do we pray? How do we pray?

"Faithful God, may we rely on you alone. May we confess with our lives that you, the Lord, are our only God."

GOD GIVES COURAGE

1 Kings 19:1–21 NIV

DAY ONE READING AND QUESTIONS

Now Ahab told Jezebel everything Elijah had done and how he had killed all the prophets with the sword. So Jezebel sent a messenger to Elijah to say, "May the gods deal with me, be it ever so severely, if by this time tomorrow I do not make your life like that of one of them."

Elijah was afraid and ran for his life. When he came to Beersheba in Judah, he left his servant there, while he himself went a day's journey into the wilderness. He came to a broom bush, sat down under it and prayed that he might die. "I have had enough, LORD," he said. "Take my life; I am no better than my ancestors."

1. *After what the Lord had done at Mount Carmel, why is Elijah afraid?*

2. *Why does Elijah want to die?*

3. *What does Elijah mean by "I am no better than my ancestors"?*

DAY TWO READING AND QUESTIONS

Then he lay down under the bush and fell asleep.

All at once an angel touched him and said, "Get up and eat." He looked around, and there by his head was some bread baked over hot coals, and a jar of water. He ate and drank and then lay down again.

The angel of the LORD came back a second time and touched him and said, "Get up and eat, for the journey is too much for you." So he got up and ate and drank. Strengthened by that food, he traveled forty days and forty nights until he reached Horeb, the mountain of God. There he went into a cave and spent the night.

And the word of the LORD came to him: "What are you doing here, Elijah?"

He replied, "I have been very zealous for the LORD God Almighty. The Israelites have rejected your covenant, torn down your altars, and put your prophets to death with the sword. I am the only one left, and now they are trying to kill me too."

1. *Why does the Lord keep feeding Elijah?*

2. *Why is Horeb (also called Sinai) called "the mountain of God"?*

3. *Why did Elijah go to Horeb?*

DAY THREE READING AND QUESTIONS

The LORD said, "Go out and stand on the mountain in the presence of the LORD, for the LORD is about to pass by."

Then a great and powerful wind tore the mountains apart and shattered the rocks before the LORD, but the LORD was not in the wind. After the wind there was an earthquake, but the

LORD was not in the earthquake. After the earthquake came a fire, but the LORD was not in the fire. And after the fire came a gentle whisper. When Elijah heard it, he pulled his cloak over his face and went out and stood at the mouth of the cave.

Then a voice said to him, "What are you doing here, Elijah?"

He replied, "I have been very zealous for the LORD God Almighty. The Israelites have rejected your covenant, torn down your altars, and put your prophets to death with the sword. I am the only one left, and now they are trying to kill me too."

1. *Who else in the Bible saw the Lord on Mount Horeb (Sinai)? What does this tell us about Elijah?*

2. *In the contest with the prophets of Baal, the Lord answered with fire. How does he answer here?*

3. *Why do you think the Lord speaks to Elijah in a gentle whisper?*

DAY FOUR READING AND QUESTIONS

The LORD said to him, "Go back the way you came, and go to the Desert of Damascus. When you get there, anoint Hazael king over Aram. Also, anoint Jehu son of Nimshi king over Israel, and anoint Elisha son of Shaphat from Abel Meholah to succeed you as prophet. Jehu will put to death any who escape the sword of Hazael, and Elisha will put to death any who escape the sword of Jehu. Yet I reserve seven thousand in Israel—all whose knees have not bowed down to Baal and whose mouths have not kissed him."

So Elijah went from there and found Elisha son of Shaphat. He was plowing with twelve yoke of oxen, and he himself was driving the twelfth pair. Elijah went up to him and threw his cloak around him. Elisha then left his oxen and ran after Elijah. "Let me kiss my father and mother goodbye," he said, "and then I will come with you."

"Go back," Elijah replied. "What have I done to you?"

So Elisha left him and went back. He took his yoke of oxen and slaughtered them. He burned the plowing equipment to cook the meat and gave it to the people, and they ate. Then he set out to follow Elijah and became his servant.

1. *Elijah is discouraged in his work as prophet. Why does the Lord give him more work to do?*

2. *What are two ways the Lord shows Elijah that he is not alone as prophet?*

3. *What does Elisha leave behind to follow Elijah?*

DAY FIVE READING AND QUESTIONS

Go back and read 1 Kings 19:1–21.

1. *After his great victory over the prophets of Baal, Elijah is profoundly discouraged. Why is it we sometimes feel alone and abandoned by God soon after "mountaintop" spiritual experiences?*

2. *By coming to Horeb (Sinai), is Elijah seeking the Lord or trying to avoid him?*

3. *Is it encouraging or discouraging to appoint one's successor?*

Meditation on 1 Kings 19:1–21

Elijah had just had a mountaintop spiritual experience with God. The Lord had given him a great victory over the prophets of Baal at Mount Carmel.

But Queen Jezebel is not happy that her prophets have been slaughtered. She threatens to kill Elijah the next day.

Then Elijah remembered the great power of God on Mount Carmel, and he knew the Lord was more powerful than Jezebel, so he was not afraid of her.

That's what we might expect if we had not read this story before. But that's not what happened. Elijah is afraid. So afraid that he runs to Beersheba at the very edge of Israel. So afraid that he asks the Lord to kill him so he will not fall into the hands of Jezebel. An angel comes to feed and comfort him. He is still afraid and runs to the desert to Mount Horeb. There the Lord appears to him, not in wind or fire or earthquake, but with a gentle whisper. He gives Elijah work to do, assuring him that he is not the only one loyal to the Lord.

Like Elijah, after mountaintop spiritual experiences, we may expect smooth sailing in our walk with God. But storms and threats come. Our faith is shaken. We feel alone. Like Elijah, even in our fear and doubt, we must listen for the gentle whisper of the Lord's reassuring voice. And we must do the work he has called us to do.

"God of wind, fire, earthquake, and the gentle whisper, open the ears of our hearts to hear your voice."

GOD PUNISHES INJUSTICE

1 Kings 21:1–29 ESV

DAY ONE READING AND QUESTIONS

Now Naboth the Jezreelite had a vineyard in Jezreel, beside the palace of Ahab king of Samaria. And after this Ahab said to Naboth, "Give me your vineyard, that I may have it for a vegetable garden, because it is near my house, and I will give you a better vineyard for it; or, if it seems good to you, I will give you its value in money." But Naboth said to Ahab, "The LORD forbid that I should give you the inheritance of my fathers." And Ahab went into his house vexed and sullen because of what Naboth the Jezreelite had said to him, for he had said, "I will not give you the inheritance of my fathers." And he lay down on his bed and turned away his face and would eat no food.

But Jezebel his wife came to him and said to him, "Why is your spirit so vexed that you eat no food?" And he said to her, "Because I spoke to Naboth the Jezreelite and said to him, 'Give me your vineyard for money, or else, if it please you, I will give you another vineyard for it.' And he answered, 'I will not give you my vineyard.'" And Jezebel his wife said to him, "Do you now govern Israel? Arise and eat bread and let your heart be cheerful; I will give you the vineyard of Naboth the Jezreelite."

1. *Why won't Naboth sell his land?*

2. *How would you describe Ahab in these verses?*

3. *How would you describe Jezebel in these verses?*

DAY TWO READING AND QUESTIONS

So she wrote letters in Ahab's name and sealed them with his seal, and she sent the letters to the elders and the leaders who lived with Naboth in his city. And she wrote in the letters, "Proclaim a fast, and set Naboth at the head of the people. And set two worthless men opposite him, and let them bring a charge against him, saying, 'You have cursed God and the king.' Then take him out and stone him to death." And the men of his city, the elders and the leaders who lived in his city, did as Jezebel had sent word to them. As it was written in the letters that she had sent to them, they proclaimed a fast and set Naboth at the head of the people. And the two worthless men came in and sat opposite him. And the worthless men brought a charge against Naboth in the presence of the people, saying, "Naboth cursed God and the king." So they took him outside the city and stoned him to death with stones. Then they sent to Jezebel, saying, "Naboth has been stoned; he is dead."

As soon as Jezebel heard that Naboth had been stoned and was dead, Jezebel said to Ahab, "Arise, take possession of the vineyard of Naboth the Jezreelite, which he refused to give you for money, for Naboth is not alive, but dead." And as soon as Ahab heard that Naboth was dead, Ahab arose to go down to the vineyard of Naboth the Jezreelite, to take possession of it.

1. *Which of the Ten Commandments are violated in this story? Why are those commandments so important?*

2. *Why did the city leaders do what Jezebel told them to do?*

3. *What gives Ahab the right to seize Naboth's land?*

DAY THREE READING AND QUESTIONS

Then the word of the LORD came to Elijah the Tishbite, saying, "Arise, go down to meet Ahab king of Israel, who is in Samaria; behold, he is in the vineyard of Naboth, where he has gone to take possession. And you shall say to him, 'Thus says the LORD, "Have you killed and also taken possession?"' And you shall say to him, 'Thus says the LORD: "In the place where dogs licked up the blood of Naboth shall dogs lick your own blood."'"

Ahab said to Elijah, "Have you found me, O my enemy?" He answered, "I have found you, because you have sold yourself to do what is evil in the sight of the LORD. Behold, I will bring disaster upon you. I will utterly burn you up, and will cut off from Ahab every male, bond or free, in Israel. And I will make your house like the house of Jeroboam the son of Nebat, and like the house of Baasha the son of Ahijah, for the anger to which you have provoked me, and because you have made Israel to sin. And of Jezebel the LORD also said, 'The dogs shall eat Jezebel within the walls of Jezreel.' Anyone belonging to Ahab who dies in the city the dogs shall eat, and anyone of his who dies in the open country the birds of the heavens shall eat."

1. *Why is Elijah no longer afraid of Ahab and Jezebel?*

2. *What crimes does Elijah accuse Ahab of committing?*

3. *What punishments does God bring on Ahab and Jezebel?*

DAY FOUR READING AND QUESTIONS

(There was none who sold himself to do what was evil in the sight of the LORD like Ahab, whom Jezebel his wife incited. He acted very abominably in going after idols, as the Amorites had done, whom the LORD cast out before the people of Israel.)

And when Ahab heard those words, he tore his clothes and put sackcloth on his flesh and fasted and lay in sackcloth and went about dejectedly. And the word of the LORD came to Elijah the Tishbite, saying, "Have you seen how Ahab has humbled himself before me? Because he has humbled himself before me, I will not bring the disaster in his days; but in his son's days I will bring the disaster upon his house."

1. *Besides cheating and killing Naboth, what other evil had Ahab done?*

2. *What was Jezebel's role in carrying out that evil?*

3. *Why does the Lord show mercy to Ahab?*

DAY FIVE READING AND QUESTIONS

Go back and read 1 Kings 21:1–29.

1. *Which sin is worse, killing Naboth or leading Israel into idolatry? Why? How are those two sins related?*

2. *Who deserves more blame, Ahab or Jezebel? Why?*

3. *Why does this story make us angry?*

Meditation on 1 Kings 21:1–29

This story makes me so mad. King Ahab wants Naboth's land, not for the good of the kingdom (as in eminent domain) but simply because he wants it for his vegetable garden. Poor Naboth does not want to sell the land that has been in his family for generations. But instead of accepting that decision, Ahab has Naboth falsely accused and killed. Or rather (since Ahab is a whining wimp), the conniving Queen Jezebel has Naboth killed. Then Ahab takes his land.

Can there be a greater injustice? This story makes the Lord angry, too. So he has Elijah announce his judgment on Ahab and Jezebel. Yet God punishes them not just for what they did to Naboth but for going after idols.

Is there a connection between the idolatry of Ahab and Jezebel and their treatment of Naboth? Yes, indeed, just as there is a connection between the idolatry and injustice of our day. If we worship the idols of our age—power, money, fame—we begin to treat people as mere objects who get in the way of our desires. And we do whatever we need to do—lie, cheat, steal, and kill—to get them out of the way. Ahab and Jezebel are still around in our world.

If the story of Naboth makes us angry but we are not moved by the stories of injustice in our world, then we need to check our lives to see what idols we follow.

"God of justice, take away our idols."

GOD SENDS HIS SPIRIT

2 Kings 2:1–25 NLT

DAY ONE READING AND QUESTIONS

When the LORD was about to take Elijah up to heaven in a whirlwind, Elijah and Elisha were traveling from Gilgal. And Elijah said to Elisha, "Stay here, for the LORD has told me to go to Bethel."

But Elisha replied, "As surely as the LORD lives and you yourself live, I will never leave you!" So they went down together to Bethel.

The group of prophets from Bethel came to Elisha and asked him, "Did you know that the LORD is going to take your master away from you today?"

"Of course I know," Elisha answered. "But be quiet about it."

Then Elijah said to Elisha, "Stay here, for the LORD has told me to go to Jericho."

But Elisha replied again, "As surely as the LORD lives and you yourself live, I will never leave you." So they went on together to Jericho.

Then the group of prophets from Jericho came to Elisha and asked him, "Did you know that the LORD is going to take your master away from you today?"

"Of course I know," Elisha answered. "But be quiet about it."

Then Elijah said to Elisha, "Stay here, for the LORD has told me to go to the Jordan River."

But again Elisha replied, "As surely as the LORD lives and you yourself live, I will never leave you." So they went on together.

1. *Why does Elijah want Elisha to stay and not go with him?*

2. *How did the prophets know about Elijah's impending death?*

3. *Why does Elisha insist on following Elijah?*

DAY TWO READING AND QUESTIONS

Fifty men from the group of prophets also went and watched from a distance as Elijah and Elisha stopped beside the Jordan River. Then Elijah folded his cloak together and struck the water with it. The river divided, and the two of them went across on dry ground!

When they came to the other side, Elijah said to Elisha, "Tell me what I can do for you before I am taken away."

And Elisha replied, "Please let me inherit a double share of your spirit and become your successor."

"You have asked a difficult thing," Elijah replied. "If you see me when I am taken from you, then you will get your request. But if not, then you won't."

As they were walking along and talking, suddenly a chariot of fire appeared, drawn by horses of fire. It drove between the two men, separating them, and Elijah was carried by a whirlwind into heaven. Elisha saw it and cried out, "My father! My father! I see the chariots and charioteers of Israel!" And as they disappeared from sight, Elisha tore his clothes in distress.

1. *Crossing the Jordan River on dry land reminds us of what two Bible stories?*

2. *Why does Elisha ask for a double portion of the Spirit?*

3. *Being taken into heaven reminds us of what New Testament story?*

DAY THREE READING AND QUESTIONS

Elisha picked up Elijah's cloak, which had fallen when he was taken up. Then Elisha returned to the bank of the Jordan River. He struck the water with Elijah's cloak and cried out, "Where is the LORD, the God of Elijah?" Then the river divided, and Elisha went across.

When the group of prophets from Jericho saw from a distance what happened, they exclaimed, "Elijah's spirit rests upon Elisha!" And they went to meet him and bowed to the ground before him. "Sir," they said, "just say the word and fifty of our strongest men will search the wilderness for your master. Perhaps the Spirit of the LORD has left him on some mountain or in some valley."

"No," Elisha said, "don't send them." But they kept urging him until they shamed him into agreeing, and he finally said, "All right, send them." So fifty men searched for three days but did not find Elijah. Elisha was still at Jericho when they returned. "Didn't I tell you not to go?" he asked.

1. *How do we know Elisha has the spirit of Elijah?*

2. *Why did the prophets want to search for Elijah?*

3. *Why does Elisha tell them not to search?*

DAY FOUR READING AND QUESTIONS

One day the leaders of the town of Jericho visited Elisha. "We have a problem, my lord," they told him. "This town is located in pleasant surroundings, as you can see. But the water is bad, and the land is unproductive."

Elisha said, "Bring me a new bowl with salt in it." So they brought it to him. Then he went out to the spring that supplied the town with water and threw the salt into it. And he said, "This is what the LORD says: I have purified this water. It will no longer cause death or infertility." And the water has remained pure ever since, just as Elisha said.

Elisha left Jericho and went up to Bethel. As he was walking along the road, a group of boys from the town began mocking and making fun of him. "Go away, baldy!" they chanted. "Go away, baldy!" Elisha turned around and looked at them, and he cursed them in the name of the LORD. Then two bears came out of the woods and mauled forty-two of them. From there Elisha went to Mount Carmel and finally returned to Samaria.

1. *What other biblical miracles come to mind when you read of the purification of the water?*

2. *Who purified the water?*

3. *Why would Elisha kill these boys for mocking him?*

DAY FIVE READING AND QUESTIONS

Go back and read 2 Kings 2:1–25.

1. *Who else in the Bible is taken up to heaven?*

2. *What is the source of Elisha's power?*

3. *Does Elisha always use that power in the right way?*

Meditation on 2 Kings 2:1–25

These verses tell one of the most amazing stories of the Bible followed by one of the most disturbing stories.

Elijah rides a fiery chariot into heaven. Amazing! Particularly amazing since in the Old Testament, those who die go down to Sheol, the place of the dead. The only other person in the Old Testament who does not seem to die is Enoch, who is "taken" by God (Gen. 5:24). No wonder the group of prophets who saw this thought the Lord had simply deposited Elijah in another place.

Elisha witnesses this great event and so is given the Spirit that rested on Elijah, allowing him to do great miracles. Elisha parts the waters as Moses, Joshua, and Elijah had done. Elisha makes bad water sweet as Moses had done. There seems to be no limit to the power given to Elisha.

Then he uses that power to bring bears to kill forty-two boys. Why? Had they worshiped other gods? Cursed the Lord? No. They had made fun of Elisha's baldness.

What are we to make of this story? Some may try to defend Elisha's action. To make fun of him, the Lord's anointed prophet, was to ridicule the Lord. But his actions are the definition of overkill.

Those who have the Spirit sometimes do horrible things. Sometimes they do those things in the name of God. We must listen to the Spirit who controls us instead of thinking we control the Spirit's power. Those who have the Spirit are called to bring life from death, as Elisha did by purifying the water. But we also can be death-dealers, all while claiming God to be on our side.

"God of power and glory, fill us with the Spirit of life."

GOD REWARDS THOSE WHO CARE FOR HIS PEOPLE

2 Kings 4:1–37 NIV

DAY ONE READING AND QUESTIONS

The wife of a man from the company of the prophets cried out to Elisha, "Your servant my husband is dead, and you know that he revered the LORD. But now his creditor is coming to take my two boys as his slaves."

Elisha replied to her, "How can I help you? Tell me, what do you have in your house?"

"Your servant has nothing there at all," she said, "except a small jar of olive oil."

Elisha said, "Go around and ask all your neighbors for empty jars. Don't ask for just a few. Then go inside and shut the door behind you and your sons. Pour oil into all the jars, and as each is filled, put it to one side."

She left him and shut the door behind her and her sons. They brought the jars to her and she kept pouring. When all the jars were full, she said to her son, "Bring me another one."

But he replied, "There is not a jar left." Then the oil stopped flowing.

She went and told the man of God, and he said, "Go, sell the oil and pay your debts. You and your sons can live on what is left."

1. *In what other Bible stories is food multiplied or changed?*

2. *Why does Elisha help this woman?*

3. *How do the neighbors help this woman?*

DAY TWO READING AND QUESTIONS

One day Elisha went to Shunem. And a well-to-do woman was there, who urged him to stay for a meal. So whenever he came by, he stopped there to eat. She said to her husband, "I know that this man who often comes our way is a holy man of God. Let's make a small room on the roof and put in it a bed and a table, a chair and a lamp for him. Then he can stay there whenever he comes to us."

One day when Elisha came, he went up to his room and lay down there. He said to his servant Gehazi, "Call the Shunammite." So he called her, and she stood before him. Elisha said to him, "Tell her, 'You have gone to all this trouble for us. Now what can be done for you? Can we speak on your behalf to the king or the commander of the army?'"

She replied, "I have a home among my own people."

"What can be done for her?" Elisha asked.

Gehazi said, "She has no son, and her husband is old."

Then Elisha said, "Call her." So he called her, and she stood in the doorway. "About this time next year," Elisha said, "you will hold a son in your arms."

"No, my lord!" she objected. "Please, man of God, don't mislead your servant!"

But the woman became pregnant, and the next year about that same time she gave birth to a son, just as Elisha had told her.

1. *Why does this woman make a place for Elisha?*

2. *What does the woman mean when she says, "I have a home among my own people"?*

3. *What other Bible stories deal with women who cannot have children?*

DAY THREE READING AND QUESTIONS

The child grew, and one day he went out to his father, who was with the reapers. He said to his father, "My head! My head!"

His father told a servant, "Carry him to his mother." After the servant had lifted him up and carried him to his mother, the boy sat on her lap until noon, and then he died. She went up and laid him on the bed of the man of God, then shut the door and went out.

She called her husband and said, "Please send me one of the servants and a donkey so I can go to the man of God quickly and return."

"Why go to him today?" he asked. "It's not the New Moon or the Sabbath."

"That's all right," she said.

She saddled the donkey and said to her servant, "Lead on; don't slow down for me unless I tell you." So she set out and came to the man of God at Mount Carmel.

When he saw her in the distance, the man of God said to his servant Gehazi, "Look! There's the Shunammite! Run to meet her and ask her, 'Are you all right? Is your husband all right? Is your child all right?'"

"Everything is all right," she said.

1. *Why is it such a tragedy that this boy died?*

2. *Why is the woman's husband surprised that she wants to go see Elisha?*

3. *Why does the woman tell Gehazi that everything is all right?*

DAY FOUR READING AND QUESTIONS

When she reached the man of God at the mountain, she took hold of his feet. Gehazi came over to push her away, but the man of God said, "Leave her alone! She is in bitter distress, but the LORD has hidden it from me and has not told me why."

"Did I ask you for a son, my lord?" she said. "Didn't I tell you, 'Don't raise my hopes'?"

Elisha said to Gehazi, "Tuck your cloak into your belt, take my staff in your hand and run. Don't greet anyone you meet, and if anyone greets you, do not answer. Lay my staff on the boy's face."

But the child's mother said, "As surely as the LORD lives and as you live, I will not leave you." So he got up and followed her.

Gehazi went on ahead and laid the staff on the boy's face, but there was no sound or response. So Gehazi went back to meet Elisha and told him, "The boy has not awakened."

When Elisha reached the house, there was the boy lying dead on his couch. He went in, shut the door on the two of them and prayed to the LORD. Then he got on the bed and lay on the boy, mouth to mouth, eyes to eyes, hands to hands. As he stretched himself out on him, the boy's body grew warm. Elisha turned away and walked back and forth in the room and then got on the bed and stretched out on him once more. The boy sneezed seven times and opened his eyes.

Elisha summoned Gehazi and said, "Call the Shunammite." And he did. When she came, he said, "Take your son." She came in, fell at his feet and bowed to the ground. Then she took her son and went out.

1. *How does Elisha know what has happened to the boy?*

2. *Why does Elisha at first send Gehazi with his staff?*

3. *What other biblical miracle does this story remind you of?*

DAY FIVE READING AND QUESTIONS

Go back and read 2 Kings 4:1–37.

1. *Why does Elisha provide for others? Why do others provide for Elisha?*

2. *What are the advantages and disadvantages of having a prophet in your house?*

3. *What is worse, to have no hope or to have your hopes dashed?*

Meditation on 2 Kings 4:1–37

"No good deed goes unpunished."

It's a cynical but, in my experience, true statement. When you go out of your way to help others, it often requires much more time, effort, and money than anticipated. Helping is often painful.

That's what this woman discovers. She makes a room for Elisha. In return, he promises her a son after she had given up all hope of having one. She is afraid to believe the prophet. "Please, man of God, don't mislead your servant!" It all seems too good to be true.

But it does come true! She has a son in her and her husband's old age, much like Abraham and Sarah. Her fondest wish has come true.

Then it all goes wrong. "My head! My head!" the boy cries. Then he dies in his mother's arms. Those who have lost children can testify to the depth of her grief. It would have been better not to have had a child. She does not know what to do except hurry to the prophet. She blames him for this tragedy. "Did I ask you for a son, my lord?" she asks. "Didn't I tell you, 'Don't raise my hopes'?" It's not clear what, if anything, she expects from Elisha.

But Elisha acts. After a false start with his staff, Elisha himself brings the boy from the dead. Or rather, the Lord gives the boy new life.

God calls us, just like this woman, to do good to the stranger, expecting no reward. Like her, sometimes we may have difficulty in trusting God because his promises seem so unbelievable. He promises our heart's desire. He gives hope where there is none. He provides for us daily. He forgives all our sins. He brings life where there can be no life. Eternal life with him.

The Lord has raised our hopes. Even when it seems those hopes are dashed, we must maintain our trust in the one who gives life.

"God of life, increase our trust in you."

GOD BLESSES THE HUMBLE

2 Kings 5:1–27 ESV

DAY ONE READING AND QUESTIONS

Naaman, commander of the army of the king of Syria, was a great man with his master and in high favor, because by him the LORD had given victory to Syria. He was a mighty man of valor, but he was a leper. Now the Syrians on one of their raids had carried off a little girl from the land of Israel, and she worked in the service of Naaman's wife. She said to her mistress, "Would that my lord were with the prophet who is in Samaria! He would cure him of his leprosy." So Naaman went in and told his lord, "Thus and so spoke the girl from the land of Israel." And the king of Syria said, "Go now, and I will send a letter to the king of Israel."

So he went, taking with him ten talents of silver, six thousand shekels of gold, and ten changes of clothing. And he brought the letter to the king of Israel, which read, "When this letter reaches you, know that I have sent to you Naaman my servant, that you may cure him of his leprosy." And when the king of Israel read the letter, he tore his clothes and said, "Am I God, to kill and to make alive, that this man sends word to me to cure a man of his leprosy? Only consider, and see how he is seeking a quarrel with me."

1. *Is it surprising that the Lord would give victory to the Syrians over Israel? Why or why not?*

2. *How does the Lord work through a nameless slave girl?*

3. *Why is the king of Israel afraid when he gets the letter from the Syrian king?*

DAY TWO READING AND QUESTIONS

But when Elisha the man of God heard that the king of Israel had torn his clothes, he sent to the king, saying, "Why have you torn your clothes? Let him come now to me, that he may know that there is a prophet in Israel." So Naaman came with his horses and chariots and stood at the door of Elisha's house. And Elisha sent a messenger to him, saying, "Go and wash in the Jordan seven times, and your flesh shall be restored, and you shall be clean." But Naaman was angry and went away, saying, "Behold, I thought that he would surely come out to me and stand and call upon the name of the LORD his God, and wave his hand over the place and cure the leper. Are not Abana and Pharpar, the rivers of Damascus, better than all the waters of Israel? Could I not wash in them and be clean?" So he turned and went away in a rage. But his servants came near and said to him, "My father, it is a great word the prophet has spoken to you; will you not do it? Has he actually said to you, 'Wash, and be clean'?" So he went down and dipped himself seven times in the Jordan, according to the word of the man of God, and his flesh was restored like the flesh of a little child, and he was clean.

1. *Why does Elisha not come out of his house and greet Naaman?*

2. *Why was Naaman angry?*

3. *Why does Naaman overcome his anger and do what Elisha says?*

DAY THREE READING AND QUESTIONS

Then he returned to the man of God, he and all his company, and he came and stood before him. And he said, "Behold, I know that there is no God in all the earth but in Israel; so accept now a present from your servant." But he said, "As the Lord lives, before whom I stand, I will receive none." And he urged him to take it, but he refused. Then Naaman said, "If not, please let there be given to your servant two mule loads of earth, for from now on your servant will not offer burnt offering or sacrifice to any god but the Lord. In this matter may the Lord pardon your servant: when my master goes into the house of Rimmon to worship there, leaning on my arm, and I bow myself in the house of Rimmon, when I bow myself in the house of Rimmon, the Lord pardon your servant in this matter." He said to him, "Go in peace."

1. *Why does Elisha refuse the present from Naaman?*

2. *Why does Naaman want to take two loads of Israelite earth back with him?*

3. *Since Naaman vows to sacrifice only to the Lord, why does he ask forgiveness for entering the temple of another god, Rimmon?*

DAY FOUR READING AND QUESTIONS

But when Naaman had gone from him a short distance, Gehazi, the servant of Elisha the man of God, said, "See, my master has spared this Naaman the Syrian, in not accepting from his hand what he brought. As the LORD lives, I will run after him and get something from him." So Gehazi followed Naaman. And when Naaman saw someone running after him, he got down from the chariot to meet him and said, "Is all well?" And he said, "All is well. My master has sent me to say, 'There have just now come to me from the hill country of Ephraim two young men of the sons of the prophets. Please give them a talent of silver and two changes of clothing.'" And Naaman said, "Be pleased to accept two talents." And he urged him and tied up two talents of silver in two bags, with two changes of clothing, and laid them on two of his servants. And they carried them before Gehazi. And when he came to the hill, he took them from their hand and put them in the house, and he sent the men away, and they departed. He went in and stood before his master, and Elisha said to him, "Where have you been, Gehazi?" And he said, "Your servant went nowhere." But he said to him, "Did not my heart go when the man turned from his chariot to meet you? Was it a time to accept money and garments, olive orchards and vineyards, sheep and oxen, male servants and female servants? Therefore the leprosy of Naaman shall cling to you and to your descendants forever." So he went out from his presence a leper, like snow.

1. *Why does Gehazi follow Naaman?*

2. *What lies does Gehazi tell?*

3. *How does Elisha know about Gehazi's actions?*

DAY FIVE READING AND QUESTIONS

Go back and read 2 Kings 5:1–27.

1. *How had Elisha healed people in other stories? How does Naaman expect to be healed?*

2. *Who healed Naaman? Who cursed Gehazi?*

3. *After years of being a faithful assistant to Elisha, why would Gehazi act the way he does?*

Meditation on 2 Kings 5:1–27

Pride. Privilege. Fame. They can mess with our heads. They can lead to a feeling of self-sufficiency. And that separates us from God and blessings.

Naaman has good reason for pride. He commands a great, victorious army. He has the respect of his king and his country.

But he has leprosy that cannot be cured. So he swallows his pride and listens to the advice from his wife's slave girl. "Would that my lord were with the prophet who is in Samaria! He would cure him of his leprosy." So

Naaman, the great commander, lowers himself to go to a foreign land to see the prophet of a foreign God.

However, perhaps thoughtlessly, he goes with the trappings of pride—great wealth and military force. Those who are privileged rarely recognize the outward signs of their privilege. A friend of mine was in a store here in Nashville when a famous country music star cut in line at the cash register. When those in line objected, she asked, "Do you know who I am?"

Perhaps that is what Naaman wants to ask Elisha. The prophet will not even leave his house for the great commander. Elisha sends a servant with instructions: seven dips in the Jordan will cure the leprosy.

How does Naaman react to this wonderful news that he can be cured? With joy? Gratitude? No. He is deeply offended and angry. *Who is this prophet to give silly instructions from a silly God? Dunk seven times in the Jordan, indeed!*

But his servants persuade him to swallow his pride. He dips into the Jordan River seven times and is cured. Even then, his pride demands that he pay for the cure. But Elisha will take no money. The Lord blesses freely.

Pride. How often has it kept us from obeying God? How often have we refused the Lord's blessings because of our sense of privilege? How often have we neglected the small daily acts of obedience the Lord has called us to because we dreamed of doing great things for God? Often, it is only when desperate, like Naaman, that we swallow our pride and receive what the Lord wants to give.

"Almighty God, humble us before you so we may obey and live."

GOD'S PEOPLE LISTEN TO HIS VOICE

2 Chronicles 24:1–22 NLT

DAY ONE READING AND QUESTIONS

Joash was seven years old when he became king, and he reigned in Jerusalem forty years. His mother was Zibiah from Beersheba. Joash did what was pleasing in the LORD's sight throughout the lifetime of Jehoiada the priest. Jehoiada chose two wives for Joash, and he had sons and daughters.

At one point Joash decided to repair and restore the Temple of the LORD. He summoned the priests and Levites and gave them these instructions: "Go to all the towns of Judah and collect the required annual offerings, so that we can repair the Temple of your God. Do not delay!" But the Levites did not act immediately.

So the king called for Jehoiada the high priest and asked him, "Why haven't you demanded that the Levites go out and collect the Temple taxes from the towns of Judah and from Jerusalem? Moses, the servant of the LORD, levied this tax on the community of Israel in order to maintain the Tabernacle of the Covenant."

1. *What makes Joash a good king?*

2. *Why do you think the temple tax had not been collected?*

3. *Are there ever good reasons for taxes?*

DAY TWO READING AND QUESTIONS

Over the years the followers of wicked Athaliah had broken into the Temple of God, and they had used all the dedicated things from the Temple of the LORD to worship the images of Baal.

So now the king ordered a chest to be made and set outside the gate leading to the Temple of the LORD. Then a proclamation was sent throughout Judah and Jerusalem, telling the people to bring to the LORD the tax that Moses, the servant of God, had required of the Israelites in the wilderness. This pleased all the leaders and the people, and they gladly brought their money and filled the chest with it.

Whenever the chest became full, the Levites would carry it to the king's officials. Then the court secretary and an officer of the high priest would come and empty the chest and take it back to the Temple again. This went on day after day, and a large amount of money was collected. The king and Jehoiada gave the money to the construction supervisors, who hired masons and carpenters to restore the Temple of the LORD. They also hired metalworkers, who made articles of iron and bronze for the LORD's Temple.

1. *Athaliah had made herself queen of Judah and promoted Baal worship (see 2 Kings 8–11 and 2 Chron. 22–23). Why was her treatment of the temple so wicked?*

2. *Why were the people happy to pay the tax?*

3. *What was done with the tax money?*

DAY THREE READING AND QUESTIONS

The men in charge of the renovation worked hard and made steady progress. They restored the Temple of God according to its original design and strengthened it. When all the repairs were finished, they brought the remaining money to the king and Jehoiada. It was used to make various articles for the Temple of the LORD—articles for worship services and for burnt offerings, including ladles and other articles made of gold and silver. And the burnt offerings were sacrificed continually in the Temple of the LORD during the lifetime of Jehoiada the priest.

Jehoiada lived to a very old age, finally dying at 130. He was buried among the kings in the City of David, because he had done so much good in Israel for God and his Temple.

But after Jehoiada's death, the leaders of Judah came and bowed before King Joash and persuaded him to listen to their advice. They decided to abandon the Temple of the LORD, the God of their ancestors, and they worshiped Asherah poles and idols instead! Because of this sin, divine anger fell on Judah and Jerusalem. Yet the LORD sent prophets to bring them back to him. The prophets warned them, but still the people would not listen.

1. *How do you think the people of Judah reacted when they saw the reconstructed temple?*

2. *Why did the people so suddenly abandon worshiping the Lord?*

3. *How does the Lord show mercy to the people?*

DAY FOUR READING AND QUESTIONS

Then the Spirit of God came upon Zechariah son of Jehoiada the priest. He stood before the people and said, "This is what God says: Why do you disobey the Lord's commands and keep yourselves from prospering? You have abandoned the Lord, and now he has abandoned you!"

Then the leaders plotted to kill Zechariah, and King Joash ordered that they stone him to death in the courtyard of the Lord's Temple. That was how King Joash repaid Jehoiada for his loyalty—by killing his son. Zechariah's last words as he died were, "May the Lord see what they are doing and avenge my death!"

1. *What is the role of the Spirit in this story?*

2. *Why do the people stone Zechariah?*

3. *Whom does Zechariah trust?*

DAY FIVE READING AND QUESTIONS

Go back and read 2 Chronicles 24:1–22.

1. *Is Joash a good king or a bad king?*

2. *Jehoiada the high priest was responsible for defeating Athaliah and placing Joash on the throne. How does that make the actions of Joash even more reprehensible?*

3. *Can you think of other examples of God's people suddenly turning against him?*

Meditation on 2 Chronicles 24:1–22

"It's not how you start; it's how you finish." This well-known expression is apt for the story of King Joash. The underlying story of Kings and Chronicles is one of Israel and Judah switching their allegiance from the Lord to other gods and back again, depending on who was king. But they never abandoned the worship of the Lord as abruptly as they do in this story.

Joash begins his reign well. He is a boy king, put on the throne by the righteous high priest Jehoiada. Joash follows Jehoiada's advice on marriage and religion. He is zealous for the Lord God, even rebuilding the temple.

And God's people follow their king. They give freely and generously to restore God's house. They rejoice at sacrificing to their God.

Then it all goes wrong. After Jehoiada dies, Joash listens to the leaders of Judah, who convince him to turn the nation back to idol worship. And despite prophetic warnings and punishment from the Lord, the people follow! When the Lord sends another prophet, Jehoiada's son Zechariah, they stone him to death.

It's almost an unbelievable story. How could God's people be so devoted to him one minute and abandon him the next?

Faith is often fragile, dependent solely on who we are with and who we listen to. In church on Sunday, surrounded by believers, we praise God fully from the heart. But the rest of the week, surrounded by scoffers who follow other "gods," we may be silent about our faith. Or we may even, like Joash and the people, listen to those voices and turn against our God.

"Faithful and merciful God, open our ears to your voice. Close our ears to those who would persuade us to abandon you."

GOD LISTENS TO HIS PEOPLE IN PRAYER

2 Kings 20:1–20 NIV

DAY ONE READING AND QUESTIONS

In those days Hezekiah became ill and was at the point of death. The prophet Isaiah son of Amoz went to him and said, "This is what the LORD says: Put your house in order, because you are going to die; you will not recover."

Hezekiah turned his face to the wall and prayed to the LORD, "Remember, LORD, how I have walked before you faithfully and with wholehearted devotion and have done what is good in your eyes." And Hezekiah wept bitterly.

1. *Why does the Lord send Isaiah to warn Hezekiah of his impending death?*

2. *Why does Hezekiah remind the Lord that he has been a faithful king?*

3. *What does Hezekiah ask God to do?*

DAY TWO READING AND QUESTIONS

Before Isaiah had left the middle court, the word of the LORD came to him: "Go back and tell Hezekiah, the ruler of my people, 'This is what the LORD, the God of your father David, says: I have heard your prayer and seen your tears; I will heal you. On the third day from now you will go up to the temple of the LORD.

I will add fifteen years to your life. And I will deliver you and this city from the hand of the king of Assyria. I will defend this city for my sake and for the sake of my servant David.'"

Then Isaiah said, "Prepare a poultice of figs." They did so and applied it to the boil, and he recovered.

Hezekiah had asked Isaiah, "What will be the sign that the LORD will heal me and that I will go up to the temple of the LORD on the third day from now?"

Isaiah answered, "This is the LORD's sign to you that the LORD will do what he has promised: Shall the shadow go forward ten steps, or shall it go back ten steps?"

"It is a simple matter for the shadow to go forward ten steps," said Hezekiah. "Rather, have it go back ten steps."

Then the prophet Isaiah called on the LORD, and the LORD made the shadow go back the ten steps it had gone down on the stairway of Ahaz.

1. *Why does the Lord heal Hezekiah?*

2. *Isaiah's prophetic message changes in a moment. Can we trust a message from God when the opposite message comes so soon?*

3. *Does asking for a sign from God show that Hezekiah has faith or lacks faith?*

DAY THREE READING AND QUESTIONS

At that time Marduk-Baladan son of Baladan king of Babylon sent Hezekiah letters and a gift, because he had heard of

Hezekiah's illness. Hezekiah received the envoys and showed them all that was in his storehouses—the silver, the gold, the spices and the fine olive oil—his armory and everything found among his treasures. There was nothing in his palace or in all his kingdom that Hezekiah did not show them.

Then Isaiah the prophet went to King Hezekiah and asked, "What did those men say, and where did they come from?"

"From a distant land," Hezekiah replied. "They came from Babylon."

The prophet asked, "What did they see in your palace?"

"They saw everything in my palace," Hezekiah said. "There is nothing among my treasures that I did not show them."

Then Isaiah said to Hezekiah, "Hear the word of the LORD: The time will surely come when everything in your palace, and all that your predecessors have stored up until this day, will be carried off to Babylon. Nothing will be left, says the LORD. And some of your descendants, your own flesh and blood who will be born to you, will be taken away, and they will become eunuchs in the palace of the king of Babylon."

1. *Why do you think Hezekiah allowed the Babylonian envoys to see everything in the palace?*

2. *Why does the Lord punish Hezekiah and Judah with Babylonian captivity?*

3. *Would it have been better for God's people for Hezekiah to have died of his illness instead of being given fifteen more years?*

DAY FOUR READING AND QUESTIONS

"The word of the LORD you have spoken is good," Hezekiah replied. For he thought, "Will there not be peace and security in my lifetime?"

As for the other events of Hezekiah's reign, all his achievements and how he made the pool and the tunnel by which he brought water into the city, are they not written in the book of the annals of the kings of Judah?

1. *Is the word of judgment from the Lord good for the people of Judah?*

2. *Why does Hezekiah think it is a good word?*

3. *What do you think about Hezekiah from these verses?*

DAY FIVE READING AND QUESTIONS

Go back and read 2 Kings 20:1–20.

1. *Can prayer change the will of God?*

2. *Should we always pray for what we want?*

3. *Is Hezekiah a good king or a bad king?*

Meditation on 2 Kings 20:1–20

Prayer can change the mind of God. That is clear from this story. God says, "Hezekiah, you will die." Hezekiah prays. God says, "Hezekiah, you will live."

Prayer can change the mind of God.

But it's not that simple. Hezekiah's prayer for life is answered, but the consequences are not good for God's people. Hezekiah's pride makes him show off all his treasures and armory to the visiting Babylonians. As a result, Babylon will conquer, enslave, and exile God's people.

When Hezekiah hears this devastating news, he is happy. At least it won't happen in his lifetime! This selfish reaction makes one wonder about the selfishness of Hezekiah's prayer.

What do we learn about prayer and about God from such a story?

Prayer can change the mind of God. But we must be very careful about changing God's mind. I am so thankful God has answered "yes" to so many of my prayers. But looking back, I'm equally thankful that he did not answer "yes" to many of them. What I asked of God in prayer seemed good and right to me at the time; but in hindsight, God granting my request would have been a disaster for me and for those I love.

In the Bible, the Lord sometimes gives his people what they ask for—a king, a child, prosperity, even longer life—not because it is good for them but as a test of their faith.

Prayer can change the mind of God. But we should not try to manipulate the will of God. We must trust that he knows best. We are encouraged to pray boldly to the God who loves us infinitely and gives good gifts to his children. But children do not always know what's best for them. They do not know that what they want may harm them and others.

So, we pray the prayer that never fails: "Your will be done."

"Listening God, give us consideration for others when we pray for what we want. We want your will above all."

GOD RESPECTS THE HEARTS OF HIS PEOPLE

2 Chronicles 30:1–27 ESV

DAY ONE READING AND QUESTIONS

Hezekiah sent to all Israel and Judah, and wrote letters also to Ephraim and Manasseh, that they should come to the house of the LORD at Jerusalem to keep the Passover to the LORD, the God of Israel. For the king and his princes and all the assembly in Jerusalem had taken counsel to keep the Passover in the second month—for they could not keep it at that time because the priests had not consecrated themselves in sufficient number, nor had the people assembled in Jerusalem—and the plan seemed right to the king and all the assembly. So they decreed to make a proclamation throughout all Israel, from Beersheba to Dan, that the people should come and keep the Passover to the LORD, the God of Israel, at Jerusalem, for they had not kept it as often as prescribed. So couriers went throughout all Israel and Judah with letters from the king and his princes, as the king had commanded, saying, "O people of Israel, return to the LORD, the God of Abraham, Isaac, and Israel, that he may turn again to the remnant of you who have escaped from the hand of the kings of Assyria. Do not be like your fathers and your brothers, who were faithless to the LORD God of their fathers, so that he made them a desolation, as you see."

1. *Passover was to be observed in the first month of the Jewish year. Why do Hezekiah and the people observe it in the second month?*

2. *What will happen if the people return to the Lord?*

3. *The "desolation" mentioned here is the exile of the northern kingdom of Israel to Assyria, which had already occurred. Why did the Lord make Israel a desolation?*

DAY TWO READING AND QUESTIONS

"Do not now be stiff-necked as your fathers were, but yield yourselves to the LORD and come to his sanctuary, which he has consecrated forever, and serve the LORD your God, that his fierce anger may turn away from you. For if you return to the LORD, your brothers and your children will find compassion with their captors and return to this land. For the LORD your God is gracious and merciful and will not turn away his face from you, if you return to him."

So the couriers went from city to city through the country of Ephraim and Manasseh, and as far as Zebulun, but they laughed them to scorn and mocked them. However, some men of Asher, of Manasseh, and of Zebulun humbled themselves and came to Jerusalem. The hand of God was also on Judah to give them one heart to do what the king and the princes commanded by the word of the LORD.

And many people came together in Jerusalem to keep the Feast of Unleavened Bread in the second month, a very great assembly. They set to work and removed the altars that were in Jerusalem, and all the altars for burning incense they took away and threw into the brook Kidron. And they slaughtered the Passover lamb on the fourteenth day of the second month. And the priests and the Levites were ashamed, so that they consecrated themselves and brought burnt offerings into the house of the LORD. They took their accustomed posts according to the Law of Moses the man of God. The priests threw the blood that they received from the hand of the Levites.

1. *Why did some laugh at the proclamation to come to Jerusalem and celebrate Passover?*

2. *Why did the people remove and throw away the altars in Jerusalem?*

3. *Why were the priests ashamed?*

DAY THREE READING AND QUESTIONS

For there were many in the assembly who had not consecrated themselves. Therefore the Levites had to slaughter the Passover lamb for everyone who was not clean, to consecrate it to the LORD. For a majority of the people, many of them from Ephraim, Manasseh, Issachar, and Zebulun, had not cleansed themselves, yet they ate the Passover otherwise than as prescribed. For Hezekiah had prayed for them, saying, "May the good LORD pardon everyone who sets his heart to seek God, the LORD, the God of his fathers, even though not according to the sanctuary's rules of cleanness." And the LORD heard Hezekiah and healed the people. And the people of Israel who were present at Jerusalem kept the Feast of Unleavened Bread seven days with great gladness, and the Levites and the priests praised the LORD day by day, singing with all their might to the LORD. And Hezekiah spoke encouragingly to all the Levites who showed good skill in the service of the LORD. So they ate the food of the festival for seven days, sacrificing peace offerings and giving thanks to the LORD, the God of their fathers.

1. *Why did some of the people eat the Passover in a way that was not prescribed by the Bible?*

2. *Why did Hezekiah think the Lord would pardon those who did not eat the Passover in the correct way?*

3. *What was the attitude of those who kept the Passover?*

DAY FOUR READING AND QUESTIONS

Then the whole assembly agreed together to keep the feast for another seven days. So they kept it for another seven days with gladness. For Hezekiah king of Judah gave the assembly 1,000 bulls and 7,000 sheep for offerings, and the princes gave the assembly 1,000 bulls and 10,000 sheep. And the priests consecrated themselves in great numbers. The whole assembly of Judah, and the priests and the Levites, and the whole assembly that came out of Israel, and the sojourners who came out of the land of Israel, and the sojourners who lived in Judah, rejoiced. So there was great joy in Jerusalem, for since the time of Solomon the son of David king of Israel there had been nothing like this in Jerusalem. Then the priests and the Levites arose and blessed the people, and their voice was heard, and their prayer came to his holy habitation in heaven.

1. *Why do the people want to extend the Passover observance?*

2. *Besides those from Judah and Israel, who else kept the Passover? Why is this significant?*

3. *Why had God's people neglected the Passover from the time of Solomon until now?*

DAY FIVE READING AND QUESTIONS

Go back and read 2 Chronicles 30:1–27.

1. *Why did the Lord give clear rules for keeping Passover and then allow his people to break those rules in these verses?*

2. *Why does God give his people rituals?*

3. *Why do God's people often neglect rituals?*

Meditation on 2 Chronicles 30:1–27

I grew up in a church that emphasized the commands of the Bible. We prided ourselves in doing Bible things in Bible ways. We even condemned other Christians for worshiping in "wrong" ways.

That pride was also mixed with fear that, try as we might, we also could be condemned by God for getting something wrong. We even heard sermons against sincerity. One could be sincere but still be punished for all eternity because one had ignorantly disobeyed God.

Hezekiah, Judah, and Israel experience a different God. He is not the God of the fine print, ready to condemn the sincerely wrong. He is the God who knows and respects the heart. So even though they celebrate Passover on the wrong day without the proper preparation and cleansing, the Lord welcomes them to the Passover table because they are doing the best they can to show their trust in him.

The table of the Lord is a feast, a banquet, a celebration! The people eat with joy and song, wanting to prolong this wonderful experience. Passover is more than keeping rules. It is communion with the God who loved their ancestors and who loves them. To paraphrase a later rabbi, "The Passover was made for humans, not humans for the Passover."

This does not mean they intentionally and willfully broke the law. It does not mean God's commands are to be taken lightly. It does show that the Lord is not a legalist. He wants all to eat with him with glad and sincere hearts.

"Lord of the banquet, feed us at your table. May all come and eat with joy."

GOD'S PEOPLE GIVE WITH JOY

2 Chronicles 31:1–21 NLT

DAY ONE READING AND QUESTIONS

When the festival ended, the Israelites who attended went to all the towns of Judah, Benjamin, Ephraim, and Manasseh, and they smashed all the sacred pillars, cut down the Asherah poles, and removed the pagan shrines and altars. After this, the Israelites returned to their own towns and homes.

Hezekiah then organized the priests and Levites into divisions to offer the burnt offerings and peace offerings, and to worship and give thanks and praise to the LORD at the gates of the Temple. The king also made a personal contribution of animals for the daily morning and evening burnt offerings, the weekly Sabbath festivals, the monthly new moon festivals, and the annual festivals as prescribed in the Law of the LORD. In addition, he required the people in Jerusalem to bring a portion of their goods to the priests and Levites, so they could devote themselves fully to the Law of the LORD.

1. *Why did the Israelites follow up the Passover by smashing idols and pagan altars?*

2. *Why did the priests and Levites need to be organized?*

3. *How did Hezekiah lead by example?*

DAY TWO READING AND QUESTIONS

When the people of Israel heard these requirements, they responded generously by bringing the first share of their grain, new wine, olive oil, honey, and all the produce of their fields. They brought a large quantity—a tithe of all they produced. The people who had moved to Judah from Israel, and the people of Judah themselves, brought in the tithes of their cattle, sheep, and goats and a tithe of the things that had been dedicated to the LORD their God, and they piled them up in great heaps. They began piling them up in late spring, and the heaps continued to grow until early autumn. When Hezekiah and his officials came and saw these huge piles, they thanked the LORD and his people Israel!

"Where did all this come from?" Hezekiah asked the priests and Levites.

And Azariah the high priest, from the family of Zadok, replied, "Since the people began bringing their gifts to the LORD's Temple, we have had enough to eat and plenty to spare. The LORD has blessed his people, and all this is left over."

1. *What motivated the Israelites to bring their tithes?*

2. *How did Hezekiah react to seeing the tithes?*

3. *What were the tithes used for?*

DAY THREE READING AND QUESTIONS

Hezekiah ordered that storerooms be prepared in the Temple of the LORD. When this was done, the people faithfully brought all the gifts, tithes, and other items dedicated for use in the Temple. Conaniah the Levite was put in charge, assisted by his brother Shimei. The supervisors under them were Jehiel, Azaziah, Nahath, Asahel, Jerimoth, Jozabad, Eliel, Ismakiah, Mahath, and Benaiah. These appointments were made by King Hezekiah and Azariah, the chief official in the Temple of God.

Kore son of Imnah the Levite, who was the gatekeeper at the East Gate, was put in charge of distributing the voluntary offerings given to God, the gifts, and the things that had been dedicated to the LORD. His faithful assistants were Eden, Miniamin, Jeshua, Shemaiah, Amariah, and Shecaniah. They distributed the gifts among the families of priests in their towns by their divisions, dividing the gifts fairly among old and young alike. They distributed the gifts to all males three years old or older, regardless of their place in the genealogical records. The distribution went to all who would come to the LORD's Temple to perform their daily duties according to their divisions.

1. *Why did they need storerooms in the temple?*

2. *What does the need for storerooms tell us about the generosity of the people?*

3. *What is the difference between tithes and voluntary gifts?*

DAY FOUR READING AND QUESTIONS

They distributed gifts to the priests who were listed by their families in the genealogical records, and to the Levites twenty years old or older who were listed according to their jobs and their divisions. Food allotments were also given to the families of all those listed in the genealogical records, including their little babies, wives, sons, and daughters. For they had all been faithful in purifying themselves.

As for the priests, the descendants of Aaron, who were living in the open villages around the towns, men were appointed by name to distribute portions to every male among the priests and to all the Levites listed in the genealogical records.

In this way, King Hezekiah handled the distribution throughout all Judah, doing what was pleasing and good in the sight of the Lord his God. In all that he did in the service of the Temple of God and in his efforts to follow God's laws and commands, Hezekiah sought his God wholeheartedly. As a result, he was very successful.

1. *Why do you think Hezekiah oversees the distribution of food?*

2. *What were all the religious reforms made by Hezekiah?*

3. *What was Hezekiah's attitude in bringing these reforms?*

DAY FIVE READING AND QUESTIONS

Go back and read 2 Chronicles 31:1–21.

1. *How does the Lord provide for the priests and Levites?*

2. *Why do you think God provides for them in this way?*

3. *Does God care about money?*

Meditation on 2 Chronicles 31:1–21

Revival!

God's people needed revival, reform, and renewal. So the Lord worked through Hezekiah to bring back the festivals, the sacrifices, and the temple.

And it took money.

Churches have the reputation of always asking for money. The most dreaded Sunday was the one with "The Sermon on the Amount," when church leaders laid out the budget for the next year and what it would take to make it. Some of those sermons almost sounded like, "The Lord needs your help. He's really short this year. Can you help the poor Guy out?"

God doesn't need your money. He didn't need it in Hezekiah's day. The Lord didn't really need a temple, but if he did, he could build and care for it himself. The priests, Levites, and their families deserved to be fed for the work they did. But the Lord could have done it by himself with manna and quail.

But he did not. He asked the other Israelites to give a tenth of their goods. He also asked for gifts above the tithe. Why?

God doesn't need our money. But he wants us. All of us. Including our gifts and money. He wants those things so we might realize that all we have comes from God and be grateful. He wants our hearts to be centered on him alone, not on money and the things money can buy.

Asking for tithes and gifts is not fundraising, as if God needs our help. Instead, asking for them is an invitation to fellowship with God and with others. And that's why we (as Israel did) give with joy.

Do we need revival? Begin with giving.

"God who owns everything, thank you for the joy of giving."

GOD SPEAKS TO HIS PEOPLE

2 Chronicles 34:1–2, 8, 14–33; 35:1–19 NIV

DAY ONE READING AND QUESTIONS

Josiah was eight years old when he became king, and he reigned in Jerusalem thirty-one years. He did what was right in the eyes of the LORD and followed the ways of his father David, not turning aside to the right or to the left. . . .

In the eighteenth year of Josiah's reign, to purify the land and the temple, he sent Shaphan son of Azaliah and Maaseiah the ruler of the city, with Joah son of Joahaz, the recorder, to repair the temple of the LORD his God. . . .

While they were bringing out the money that had been taken into the temple of the LORD, Hilkiah the priest found the Book of the Law of the LORD that had been given through Moses. Hilkiah said to Shaphan the secretary, "I have found the Book of the Law in the temple of the LORD." He gave it to Shaphan.

Then Shaphan took the book to the king and reported to him: "Your officials are doing everything that has been committed to them. They have paid out the money that was in the temple of the LORD and have entrusted it to the supervisors and workers." Then Shaphan the secretary informed the king, "Hilkiah the priest has given me a book." And Shaphan read from it in the presence of the king.

When the king heard the words of the Law, he tore his robes. He gave these orders to Hilkiah, Ahikam son of Shaphan, Abdon son of Micah, Shaphan the secretary and Asaiah the king's attendant: "Go and inquire of the LORD for me and for the remnant in Israel and Judah about what is written in this book that has been found. Great is the LORD's anger that is poured out on us because those who have gone before us have not kept the word of the LORD; they have not acted in accordance with all that is written in this book."

1. *What was the Book of the Law that was found in the temple?*

2. *How could Judah and Israel have gone years without knowing what was in the Book of the Law?*

3. *Why does King Josiah tear his robes when he hears the words of the law?*

DAY TWO READING AND QUESTIONS

Hilkiah and those the king had sent with him went to speak to the prophet Huldah, who was the wife of Shallum son of Tokhath, the son of Hasrah, keeper of the wardrobe. She lived in Jerusalem, in the New Quarter.

She said to them, "This is what the LORD, the God of Israel, says: Tell the man who sent you to me, 'This is what the LORD says: I am going to bring disaster on this place and its people—all the curses written in the book that has been read in the presence of the king of Judah. Because they have forsaken me and burned incense to other gods and aroused my anger by all that their hands have made, my anger will be poured out on this place and will not be quenched.' Tell the king of Judah, who sent you to inquire of the LORD, 'This is what the LORD, the God of Israel, says concerning the words you heard: Because your heart was responsive and you humbled yourself before God when you heard what he spoke against this place and its people, and because you humbled yourself before me and tore your robes and wept in my presence, I have heard you, declares the LORD. Now I will gather you to your ancestors, and you will be buried in peace. Your eyes will not see all the disaster I am going to bring on this place and on those who live here.'"

So they took her answer back to the king.

1. *Is it surprising to find the Lord speaking through a female prophet? Why or why not?*

2. *Why will the Lord punish Judah?*

3. *Why did the Lord spare Josiah from seeing that punishment?*

DAY THREE READING AND QUESTIONS

Then the king called together all the elders of Judah and Jerusalem. He went up to the temple of the LORD with the people of Judah, the inhabitants of Jerusalem, the priests and the Levites—all the people from the least to the greatest. He read in their hearing all the words of the Book of the Covenant, which had been found in the temple of the LORD. The king stood by his pillar and renewed the covenant in the presence of the LORD—to follow the LORD and keep his commands, statutes and decrees with all his heart and all his soul, and to obey the words of the covenant written in this book.

Then he had everyone in Jerusalem and Benjamin pledge themselves to it; the people of Jerusalem did this in accordance with the covenant of God, the God of their ancestors.

Josiah removed all the detestable idols from all the territory belonging to the Israelites, and he had all who were present in Israel serve the LORD their God. As long as he lived, they did not fail to follow the LORD, the God of their ancestors.

Josiah celebrated the Passover to the LORD in Jerusalem, and the Passover lamb was slaughtered on the fourteenth day of the first month. He appointed the priests to their duties and encouraged them in the service of the LORD's temple. He said to the Levites, who instructed all Israel and who had been consecrated to the LORD: "Put the sacred ark in the temple that Solomon son of David king of Israel built. It is not to be carried about on your shoulders. Now serve the LORD your God and his people Israel. Prepare yourselves by families in your divisions, according to the instructions written by David king of Israel and by his son Solomon.

"Stand in the holy place with a group of Levites for each subdivision of the families of your fellow Israelites, the lay people. Slaughter the Passover lambs, consecrate yourselves and prepare the lambs for your fellow Israelites, doing what the LORD commanded through Moses."

1. *Why does the king read the book to the people?*

2. *How do the people react to hearing the book?*

3. *Why does Josiah give specific instructions on how to keep the Passover and where to put the ark?*

DAY FOUR READING AND QUESTIONS

Josiah provided for all the lay people who were there a total of thirty thousand lambs and goats for the Passover offerings, and also three thousand cattle—all from the king's own possessions.

His officials also contributed voluntarily to the people and the priests and Levites. Hilkiah, Zechariah and Jehiel, the officials in charge of God's temple, gave the priests twenty-six hundred Passover offerings and three hundred cattle. Also Konaniah along with Shemaiah and Nethanel, his brothers, and Hashabiah, Jeiel and Jozabad, the leaders of the Levites, provided five thousand Passover offerings and five hundred head of cattle for the Levites.

The service was arranged and the priests stood in their places with the Levites in their divisions as the king had ordered. The Passover lambs were slaughtered, and the priests splashed against the altar the blood handed to them, while the Levites skinned the animals. They set aside the burnt offerings to give them to the subdivisions of the families of the people to offer to the LORD, as it is written in the Book of Moses. They did the same with the cattle. They roasted the Passover animals over the fire as prescribed, and boiled the holy offerings in pots, caldrons and pans and served them quickly to all the people. After this, they made preparations for themselves and for the priests, because the priests, the descendants of Aaron, were sacrificing the burnt offerings and the fat portions until nightfall. So the Levites made preparations for themselves and for the Aaronic priests.

The musicians, the descendants of Asaph, were in the places prescribed by David, Asaph, Heman and Jeduthun the king's seer. The gatekeepers at each gate did not need to leave their posts, because their fellow Levites made the preparations for them.

So at that time the entire service of the LORD was carried out for the celebration of the Passover and the offering of burnt offerings on the altar of the LORD, as King Josiah had ordered. The Israelites who were present celebrated the Passover at that time and observed the Festival of Unleavened Bread for seven days. The Passover had not been observed like this in Israel since the days of the prophet Samuel; and none of the kings of Israel had ever celebrated such a Passover as did Josiah, with the priests, the Levites and all Judah and Israel who were there with the people of Jerusalem. This Passover was celebrated in the eighteenth year of Josiah's reign.

1. *Why is it significant that the king and other officials donated animals for the Passover?*

2. *How long had it been since a Passover had been celebrated like this? Why had it been so long?*

3. *Why is David mentioned in these verses?*

DAY FIVE READING AND QUESTIONS

Go back and read 2 Chronicles 34:1–2, 8, 14–33; 35:1–19.

1. *Is it good to have a Book of the Law? Why or why not?*

2. *Now that Judah has returned to the Lord, why does the Lord still promise to punish them?*

3. *Was Josiah a good king or a bad king? Why?*

Meditation on 2 Chronicles 34:1–2, 8, 14–33; 35:1–19

How can a people misplace a book from God?

Most scholars think the Book of the Law found here is some version of Deuteronomy, the "second giving of the Law" from Moses. How could God's people lose a book from Moses? By not passing down the faith to their children, the very thing Deuteronomy commands (see Deut. 6:1–9). It only takes a generation to forget the Lord God and his instructions to his people.

So, is following the Lord all about following the law? No. As we saw in the Hezekiah reform, God is not a legalistic "God of the fine print," eager to condemn his people for small faults. In this story, the Lord respects the sincere humility and actions of King Josiah.

But this story of Josiah's reform reminds us that God's people are called to take his instruction seriously. Passover, sacrifices, and temple worship are not mere outward rituals to be done correctly. They are ways God's people show their loyalty to the covenant and to the Lord as the only God and King.

It is good to have instruction from the Lord. It is a blessing, not a burden, to have a Book of the Law. Otherwise, we are left on our own with no instruction from the God who loves us. The Book is meant to lead God's people to heartfelt obedience and gratitude.

"God who speaks, open our ears to hear and obey."

GOD SEPARATES HIS PEOPLE

Ezra 3:1–13; 9:1–10:5 ESV

DAY ONE READING AND QUESTIONS

When the seventh month came, and the children of Israel were in the towns, the people gathered as one man to Jerusalem. Then arose Jeshua the son of Jozadak, with his fellow priests, and Zerubbabel the son of Shealtiel with his kinsmen, and they built the altar of the God of Israel, to offer burnt offerings on it, as it is written in the Law of Moses the man of God. They set the altar in its place, for fear was on them because of the peoples of the lands, and they offered burnt offerings on it to the LORD, burnt offerings morning and evening. And they kept the Feast of Booths, as it is written, and offered the daily burnt offerings by number according to the rule, as each day required, and after that the regular burnt offerings, the offerings at the new moon and at all the appointed feasts of the LORD, and the offerings of everyone who made a freewill offering to the LORD. From the first day of the seventh month they began to offer burnt offerings to the LORD. But the foundation of the temple of the LORD was not yet laid. So they gave money to the masons and the carpenters, and food, drink, and oil to the Sidonians and the Tyrians to bring cedar trees from Lebanon to the sea, to Joppa, according to the grant that they had from Cyrus king of Persia.

1. *Jeshua is a priest and Zerubbabel is a descendant of David. Why is it important that these two were the leaders of this revival?*

2. *Why was it important that the altar be built before the temple was reconstructed?*

3. *Why is it important that foreigners were involved in rebuilding the temple?*

DAY TWO READING AND QUESTIONS

Now in the second year after their coming to the house of God at Jerusalem, in the second month, Zerubbabel the son of Shealtiel and Jeshua the son of Jozadak made a beginning, together with the rest of their kinsmen, the priests and the Levites and all who had come to Jerusalem from the captivity. They appointed the Levites, from twenty years old and upward, to supervise the work of the house of the LORD. And Jeshua with his sons and his brothers, and Kadmiel and his sons, the sons of Judah, together supervised the workmen in the house of God, along with the sons of Henadad and the Levites, their sons and brothers.

And when the builders laid the foundation of the temple of the LORD, the priests in their vestments came forward with trumpets, and the Levites, the sons of Asaph, with cymbals, to praise the LORD, according to the directions of David king of Israel. And they sang responsively, praising and giving thanks to the LORD,

"For he is good,
for his steadfast love endures forever toward Israel."

And all the people shouted with a great shout when they praised the LORD, because the foundation of the house of the

> LORD was laid. But many of the priests and Levites and heads of fathers' houses, old men who had seen the first house, wept with a loud voice when they saw the foundation of this house being laid, though many shouted aloud for joy, so that the people could not distinguish the sound of the joyful shout from the sound of the people's weeping, for the people shouted with a great shout, and the sound was heard far away.

1. *Who had given instructions on the music of the temple? Why is this significant?*

2. *Why did some shout when the temple foundation was laid?*

3. *Why did some weep when the foundation was laid?*

DAY THREE READING AND QUESTIONS

> After these things had been done, the officials approached me and said, "The people of Israel and the priests and the Levites have not separated themselves from the peoples of the lands with their abominations, from the Canaanites, the Hittites, the Perizzites, the Jebusites, the Ammonites, the Moabites, the Egyptians, and the Amorites. For they have taken some of their daughters to be wives for themselves and for their sons, so that the holy race has mixed itself with the peoples of the lands. And in this faithlessness the hand of the officials and chief men has been foremost." As soon as I heard this, I tore my garment and my cloak and pulled hair from my head and beard and sat appalled. Then all who trembled at the words of the God of Israel, because of the faithlessness of the returned

exiles, gathered around me while I sat appalled until the evening sacrifice. And at the evening sacrifice I rose from my fasting, with my garment and my cloak torn, and fell upon my knees and spread out my hands to the LORD my God, saying:

"O my God, I am ashamed and blush to lift my face to you, my God, for our iniquities have risen higher than our heads, and our guilt has mounted up to the heavens. From the days of our fathers to this day we have been in great guilt. And for our iniquities we, our kings, and our priests have been given into the hand of the kings of the lands, to the sword, to captivity, to plundering, and to utter shame, as it is today. But now for a brief moment favor has been shown by the LORD our God, to leave us a remnant and to give us a secure hold within his holy place, that our God may brighten our eyes and grant us a little reviving in our slavery. For we are slaves. Yet our God has not forsaken us in our slavery, but has extended to us his steadfast love before the kings of Persia, to grant us some reviving to set up the house of our God, to repair its ruins, and to give us protection in Judea and Jerusalem."

1. *Why was it so important for the people of Israel not to marry foreigners?*

2. *What attitude does Ezra take in prayer?*

3. *Who led the revival among God's people?*

DAY FOUR READING AND QUESTIONS

"And now, O our God, what shall we say after this? For we have forsaken your commandments, which you commanded by your servants the prophets, saying, 'The land that you are entering, to take possession of it, is a land impure with the impurity of the peoples of the lands, with their abominations that have filled it from end to end with their uncleanness. Therefore do not give your daughters to their sons, neither take their daughters for your sons, and never seek their peace or prosperity, that you may be strong and eat the good of the land and leave it for an inheritance to your children forever.' And after all that has come upon us for our evil deeds and for our great guilt, seeing that you, our God, have punished us less than our iniquities deserved and have given us such a remnant as this, shall we break your commandments again and intermarry with the peoples who practice these abominations? Would you not be angry with us until you consumed us, so that there should be no remnant, nor any to escape? O LORD, the God of Israel, you are just, for we are left a remnant that has escaped, as it is today. Behold, we are before you in our guilt, for none can stand before you because of this."

While Ezra prayed and made confession, weeping and casting himself down before the house of God, a very great assembly of men, women, and children, gathered to him out of Israel, for the people wept bitterly. And Shecaniah the son of Jehiel, of the sons of Elam, addressed Ezra: "We have broken faith with our God and have married foreign women from the peoples of the land, but even now there is hope for Israel in spite of this. Therefore let us make a covenant with our God to put away all these wives and their children, according to the counsel of my lord and of those who tremble at the commandment of our God, and let it be done according to the Law. Arise, for it is

> your task, and we are with you; be strong and do it." Then Ezra arose and made the leading priests and Levites and all Israel take an oath that they would do as had been said. So they took the oath.

1. *Does Ezra think God is just in punishing his people?*

2. *What is Ezra afraid God will do if the people do not repent?*

3. *What is the hope in these verses?*

DAY FIVE READING AND QUESTIONS

Go back and read Ezra 3:1–13; 9:1–10:5.

1. *What do the people do to return to the Lord in these verses?*

2. *What are some Bible stories that tell of Israelites marrying foreigners?*

3. *Should God's people remain separate from others?*

Meditation on Ezra 3:1–13; 9:1–10:5

The revival led by Jeshua, Zerubbabel, and Ezra is similar to the revivals mentioned in Kings and Chronicles. God's people put away foreign gods, rebuild the altar, offer sacrifices, renew the temple, and pledge to keep the covenant.

But one thing keeps them from reconciliation with the Lord. They continue to intermarry with the people of the nations around them. So Ezra leads them to send away those wives and children.

Can that be right? The Lord wants them to break up families? Wasn't Israel to be a light to other nations? How can they influence those nations if they have no connection to them? And how about the biblical stories of foreign wives who turn to the Lord—Rahab, Ruth, and others? Why does the Lord (or at least Ezra) demand such a radical step?

I don't have the answers to these questions. But we must not let them obscure the good news in Ezra. There is hope for Israel. The Lord has allowed a remnant to return to the land. They are surrounded by hostile nations who want them to abandon their God and leave the land. Just as we are sometimes stricter with our children when they are in danger, so too the Lord protects his people.

God's people always struggle between the clear biblical teaching to avoid evil companions and the equally clear teaching that we are to be salt and light to the world. What we can be sure of is that God loves the world. If he calls us at times to be somewhat separate, it is not so we will condemn others but so we can properly love our neighbor.

"God of the nations, give us wisdom to know how to help your world."

GOD WANTS HIS PEOPLE TO LISTEN AND OBEY

Nehemiah 8:1–12; 10:28–39 NLT

DAY ONE READING AND QUESTIONS

In October, when the Israelites had settled in their towns, all the people assembled with a unified purpose at the square just inside the Water Gate. They asked Ezra the scribe to bring out the Book of the Law of Moses, which the LORD had given for Israel to obey.

So on October 8 Ezra the priest brought the Book of the Law before the assembly, which included the men and women and all the children old enough to understand. He faced the square just inside the Water Gate from early morning until noon and read aloud to everyone who could understand. All the people listened closely to the Book of the Law.

Ezra the scribe stood on a high wooden platform that had been made for the occasion. To his right stood Mattithiah, Shema, Anaiah, Uriah, Hilkiah, and Maaseiah. To his left stood Pedaiah, Mishael, Malkijah, Hashum, Hashbaddanah, Zechariah, and Meshullam. Ezra stood on the platform in full view of all the people. When they saw him open the book, they all rose to their feet.

1. *Why was public reading of the law important?*

2. *Why do you think the text lists the men standing with Ezra?*

3. *Why did the people stand when the book was read?*

DAY TWO READING AND QUESTIONS

Then Ezra praised the LORD, the great God, and all the people chanted, "Amen! Amen!" as they lifted their hands. Then they bowed down and worshiped the LORD with their faces to the ground.

The Levites—Jeshua, Bani, Sherebiah, Jamin, Akkub, Shabbethai, Hodiah, Maaseiah, Kelita, Azariah, Jozabad, Hanan, and Pelaiah—then instructed the people in the Law while everyone remained in their places. They read from the Book of the Law of God and clearly explained the meaning of what was being read, helping the people understand each passage.

Then Nehemiah the governor, Ezra the priest and scribe, and the Levites who were interpreting for the people said to them, "Don't mourn or weep on such a day as this! For today is a sacred day before the LORD your God." For the people had all been weeping as they listened to the words of the Law.

And Nehemiah continued, "Go and celebrate with a feast of rich foods and sweet drinks, and share gifts of food with people who have nothing prepared. This is a sacred day before our Lord. Don't be dejected and sad, for the joy of the LORD is your strength!"

And the Levites, too, quieted the people, telling them, "Hush! Don't weep! For this is a sacred day." So the people went away to eat and drink at a festive meal, to share gifts of food, and to celebrate with great joy because they had heard God's words and understood them.

1. *Why do the Levites need to explain the law?*

2. *Why do the people weep when they understand the law?*

3. *Why do Nehemiah and the Levites tell the people to feast instead of weeping?*

DAY THREE READING AND QUESTIONS

Then the rest of the people—the priests, Levites, gatekeepers, singers, Temple servants, and all who had separated themselves from the pagan people of the land in order to obey the Law of God, together with their wives, sons, daughters, and all who were old enough to understand—joined their leaders and bound themselves with an oath. They swore a curse on themselves if they failed to obey the Law of God as issued by his servant Moses. They solemnly promised to carefully follow all the commands, regulations, and decrees of the LORD our Lord:

> "We promise not to let our daughters marry the pagan people of the land, and not to let our sons marry their daughters.
>
> "We also promise that if the people of the land should bring any merchandise or grain to be sold on the Sabbath or on any other holy day, we will refuse to buy it. Every seventh year we will let our land rest, and we will cancel all debts owed to us.
>
> "In addition, we promise to obey the command to pay the annual Temple tax of one-eighth of an ounce of silver for the care of the Temple of our God. This will provide for the Bread of the Presence; for the regular grain offerings and burnt offerings; for the offerings on the Sabbaths, the new moon celebrations, and the annual festivals; for the holy

offerings; and for the sin offerings to make atonement for Israel. It will provide for everything necessary for the work of the Temple of our God.

"We have cast sacred lots to determine when—at regular times each year—the families of the priests, Levites, and the common people should bring wood to God's Temple to be burned on the altar of the LORD our God, as is written in the Law."

1. *What is the difference between an oath and a promise?*

2. *What specific promises do the people make?*

3. *Why do you think they make these promises?*

DAY FOUR READING AND QUESTIONS

"We promise to bring the first part of every harvest to the LORD's Temple year after year—whether it be a crop from the soil or from our fruit trees. We agree to give God our oldest sons and the firstborn of all our herds and flocks, as prescribed in the Law. We will present them to the priests who minister in the Temple of our God. We will store the produce in the storerooms of the Temple of our God. We will bring the best of our flour and other grain offerings, the best of our fruit, and the best of our new wine and olive oil. And we promise to bring to the Levites a tenth of everything our land produces, for it is the Levites who collect the tithes in all our rural towns.

"A priest—a descendant of Aaron—will be with the Levites as they receive these tithes. And a tenth of all that is collected as tithes will be delivered by the Levites to the Temple of our God and placed in the storerooms. The people and the Levites must bring these offerings of grain, new wine, and olive oil to the storerooms and place them in the sacred containers near the ministering priests, the gatekeepers, and the singers.

"We promise together not to neglect the Temple of our God."

1. *Why was it important to give the tithe?*

2. *Why was it important for a priest to receive the tithes?*

3. *Why was it important for the people not to neglect the temple?*

DAY FIVE READING AND QUESTIONS

Go back and read Nehemiah 8:1–12; 10:28–39.

1. *Why was it so important for God's people to hear and understand the law?*

2. *How should we listen to the Word of God?*

3. *How do we show we understand God's Word?*

Meditation on Nehemiah 8:1–12; 10:28–39

How do we know when someone understands the Word of God?

For years I taught the Bible in Christian schools and universities. How did I know when my students understood the Bible? When they passed the tests.

So it is with the Lord. But the tests he gives do not have multiple choice, true-or-false, or even discussion questions. The test is this: Do we do what the Lord says?

So here the heart of Ezra's revival is not the building of the city walls, or the altar, or even the temple. It is the rebuilding of an obedient people. When Ezra reads to the people the book from God, they stand in reverence, they raise hands in joy, and they bow in worship. They listen closely to the Levites who explain how the law pertains to their current situation. At first, they react with tears because they and their ancestors have not kept the law. But they are told the Word of God is good news, a time for feasting and celebration.

What's more, the people make solemn promises and vows to do what the Lord commands. They pledge their time, goods, money, and hearts.

How do we react to Scripture? With boredom? Fear? Guilt? Or do we hear it as a Word from the God who wants a relationship with us? Is Bible study a time for celebration? Do we hear and obey?

"God who speaks, may we hear and obey."

GOD SAVES HIS PEOPLE

Esther 4:10–5:14; 7:1–10 NIV

DAY ONE READING AND QUESTIONS

Then she instructed him to say to Mordecai, "All the king's officials and the people of the royal provinces know that for any man or woman who approaches the king in the inner court without being summoned the king has but one law: that they be put to death unless the king extends the gold scepter to them and spares their lives. But thirty days have passed since I was called to go to the king."

When Esther's words were reported to Mordecai, he sent back this answer: "Do not think that because you are in the king's house you alone of all the Jews will escape. For if you remain silent at this time, relief and deliverance for the Jews will arise from another place, but you and your father's family will perish. And who knows but that you have come to your royal position for such a time as this?"

Then Esther sent this reply to Mordecai: "Go, gather together all the Jews who are in Susa, and fast for me. Do not eat or drink for three days, night or day. I and my attendants will fast as you do. When this is done, I will go to the king, even though it is against the law. And if I perish, I perish."

So Mordecai went away and carried out all of Esther's instructions.

On the third day Esther put on her royal robes and stood in the inner court of the palace, in front of the king's hall. The king was sitting on his royal throne in the hall, facing the entrance. When he saw Queen Esther standing in the court, he was pleased with her and held out to her the gold scepter that was in his hand. So Esther approached and touched the tip of the scepter.

Then the king asked, "What is it, Queen Esther? What is your request? Even up to half the kingdom, it will be given you."

"If it pleases the king," replied Esther, "let the king, together with Haman, come today to a banquet I have prepared for him."

"Bring Haman at once," the king said, "so that we may do what Esther asks."

So the king and Haman went to the banquet Esther had prepared. As they were drinking wine, the king again asked Esther, "Now what is your petition? It will be given you. And what is your request? Even up to half the kingdom, it will be granted."

Esther replied, "My petition and my request is this: If the king regards me with favor and if it pleases the king to grant my petition and fulfill my request, let the king and Haman come tomorrow to the banquet I will prepare for them. Then I will answer the king's question."

1. *Haman was a Persian official who had plotted to kill all the Jews because Mordecai, Esther's uncle, refused to bow down to him (see Esther 3:1–15). Mordecai heard of the plot and sent word of it to Esther. Why is Esther reluctant to help?*

2. *Mordecai tells Esther, "And who knows but that you have come to your royal position for such a time as this?" What does this say about how God works to save his people?*

3. *Why do you think Esther invites the king and Haman to a second banquet instead of making her request?*

DAY TWO READING AND QUESTIONS

Haman went out that day happy and in high spirits. But when he saw Mordecai at the king's gate and observed that he neither rose nor showed fear in his presence, he was filled with rage against Mordecai. Nevertheless, Haman restrained himself and went home.

Calling together his friends and Zeresh, his wife, Haman boasted to them about his vast wealth, his many sons, and all the ways the king had honored him and how he had elevated him above the other nobles and officials. "And that's not all," Haman added. "I'm the only person Queen Esther invited to accompany the king to the banquet she gave. And she has invited me along with the king tomorrow. But all this gives me no satisfaction as long as I see that Jew Mordecai sitting at the king's gate."

His wife Zeresh and all his friends said to him, "Have a pole set up, reaching to a height of fifty cubits, and ask the king in the morning to have Mordecai impaled on it. Then go with the king to the banquet and enjoy yourself." This suggestion delighted Haman, and he had the pole set up.

1. *What ruins Haman's joy at being invited to the king and queen's banquet?*

2. *What do you think of Zeresh, Haman's wife, and of his friends?*

3. *Why does Haman want such a gruesome death for Mordecai?*

DAY THREE READING AND QUESTIONS

So the king and Haman went to Queen Esther's banquet, and as they were drinking wine on the second day, the king again asked, "Queen Esther, what is your petition? It will be given you. What is your request? Even up to half the kingdom, it will be granted."

Then Queen Esther answered, "If I have found favor with you, Your Majesty, and if it pleases you, grant me my life—this is my petition. And spare my people—this is my request. For I and my people have been sold to be destroyed, killed and annihilated. If we had merely been sold as male and female slaves, I would have kept quiet, because no such distress would justify disturbing the king."

King Xerxes asked Queen Esther, "Who is he? Where is he—the man who has dared to do such a thing?"

Esther said, "An adversary and enemy! This vile Haman!"

Then Haman was terrified before the king and queen. The king got up in a rage, left his wine and went out into the palace garden. But Haman, realizing that the king had already decided his fate, stayed behind to beg Queen Esther for his life.

1. *Why do you think Esther first asks the king to spare her life before asking him to spare her people?*

2. *How does Esther describe Haman?*

3. *Why does the king leave the room when he hears this?*

DAY FOUR READING AND QUESTIONS

Just as the king returned from the palace garden to the banquet hall, Haman was falling on the couch where Esther was reclining.

The king exclaimed, "Will he even molest the queen while she is with me in the house?"

As soon as the word left the king's mouth, they covered Haman's face. Then Harbona, one of the eunuchs attending the king, said, "A pole reaching to a height of fifty cubits stands by Haman's house. He had it set up for Mordecai, who spoke up to help the king."

The king said, "Impale him on it!" So they impaled Haman on the pole he had set up for Mordecai. Then the king's fury subsided.

1. *Why had Haman approached Esther? What did the king think Haman was doing?*

2. *Why do they cover Haman's face?*

3. *Why is the method of Haman's execution so appropriate?*

DAY FIVE READING AND QUESTIONS

Go back and read Esther 4:10–5:14; 7:1–10.

1. *What do you think about Mordecai from this story?*

2. *What do you think of Esther?*

3. *What is God's role in this story?*

Meditation on Esther 4:10–5:14; 7:1–10

"For such a time as this."

Most think these are the key words in Esther. Her uncle Mordecai uses these words to convince her that the Lord has made her queen at this time to save her people. God is therefore working all the time behind the scenes to do his will (what some call "providence").

I wonder if the more profound words from Mordecai come right before those famous words: "Do not think that because you are in the king's house you alone of all the Jews will escape. For if you remain silent at this time, relief and deliverance for the Jews will arise from another place, but you and your father's family will perish."

"Relief and deliverance for the Jews will arise from another place." What faith it took for Mordecai to say these words. In a time when the Jews were in exile, when no word from the Lord had come for a while, when there were no prophets doing great miracles, Mordecai still trusts that the Lord will make a way to save.

And his words remind us of our place in God's plan. Sometimes we may think it is all up to us to make sure the Lord's will is done. We pride ourselves in doing great things for God. "God has no hands but our hands."

The truth is God can work his will without us. He will bring deliverance from someone else. But we do not want him to do it without us. Like Esther, we are privileged to work with God to save his people. Yet we must always remember that it is the Lord who saves, not our wisdom, plans, or power.

"Saving God, work through us to do your will."